LESSONS

FROM THE

HEAD'S OFFICE

LESSONS

LESSONS

FROM THE

HEAD'S OFFICE

BRIAN WALTON

A SAGE Publishing Company

SAGE Publications Ltd
1 Oliver's Yard
55 City Road
London EC1Y 1SP

CORWIN
A SAGE company
2455 Teller Road
Thousand Oaks, California 91320
(800)233-9936
www.corwin.com

SAGE Publications India Pvt Ltd
B 1/I 1 Mohan Cooperative Industrial Area
Mathura Road
New Delhi 110 044

SAGE Publications Asia-Pacific Pte Ltd
3 Church Street
#10-04 Samsung Hub
Singapore 049483

Editor: James Clark
Assistant editor: Diana Alves
Production editor: Nicola Marshall
Copyeditor: Tom Bedford
Proofreader: Leigh Smithson
Indexer: Silvia Benvenuto
Marketing manager: Dilhara Attygalle
Cover design: Wendy Scott
Typeset by: C&M Digitals (P) Ltd, Chennai, India
Printed in the UK

Library of Congress Control Number: 2022949745

British Library Cataloguing in Publication data

A catalogue record for this book is available from the British Library

ISBN 978-1-5297-6772-8
ISBN 978-1-5297-6771-1 (pbk)

At SAGE we take sustainability seriously. Most of our products are printed in the UK using responsibly sourced papers and boards. When we print overseas we ensure sustainable papers are used as measured by the Book Chain Projects grading system. We undertake an annual audit to monitor our sustainability.

Contents

Contents

About the Author

Brian has worked in education for almost 30 years (and still counting) – almost 20 of them as a head teacher. He hated school and left with no qualifications, wanting to be a rock star, and ran a record shop (Madhouse Music) for a little while in his late teens. But destiny and a 'sliding doors' moment at Bridgwater College, Somerset meant that Brian, aged 20, got onto an Access to Education course (a 1990s thing that helped people with no formal qualifications get into university) despite never once thinking about becoming a teacher – he has never looked back.

He has worked in education across the South of England and currently 'head teaches' in the West Country. He is a bit of a board game geek and loves cycling, music and his very small group of friends. He is married to his lifelong best friend; they have two amazing children, and two cats (who hate him).

Acknowledgements

I owe so many people for the fact I ever became a teacher, never mind a head teacher. Those who took chances on me, pushed me or believed in me are too many to name and to miss any one of them out would be criminal. *I thank you all – you know who you are.*

In particular – Timmy and Tommy for a lifetime of challenge, laughs and friendship.

Stuart – a true educational professional who helped shape this book with words of wisdom and great insight.

I dedicate this book to my family:

My father – I miss your wisdom daily.

Mother – your warmth never leaves me.

Boo – thank you.

Julia – I could never have done what I do without you.

Foreword

There are multitudes of books about theories of leadership. Many are worthwhile, but they are frequently dry or too abstract to be of much use. There are an even bigger number of books written by famous leaders or by those who have been successful in the business world telling us the secrets of their huge achievements and how, if only we could somehow lead like them, we might be just as successful. These books sometimes inspire but they mainly depress the reader. Brian Walton's book is not one of those books. He doesn't set out with a theory of leadership (though *rebellious leadership* gets a refreshing analysis and he clearly has an intense dislike of '*leadershit*'). Nor does he tell us how wonderful he is. At its heart, this is an honest, down-to-earth, practical book, full of ideas and wisdom but without the platitudes and without the unhealthily big ego.

Why is it that most books written by leaders about their own leadership are published long after they have retired and left the scene? I think it is mainly because we are more likely to have the time to reflect and write when we are not in the middle of leading an organisation (that was certainly my experience). But it is probably also because it is easier to be honest about things after the event. Leaders can find it difficult to admit weaknesses or to talk about mistakes or how hard things are while they are still doing the job. We worry that if we talk or write about leadership while we are still leading, then we may damage our credibility or we may be setting ourselves up to fail in the future. I remember talking to a good friend once who was offered a knighthood but decided not to take it. I asked him why and he said 'What if I mess up in my next leadership role? I would feel like a fraud'.

What is so remarkable and impressive about Brian Walton's book is that he is writing about his leadership journey **while he is still on it**.

In their excellent book *Why Should Anyone Be Led by You?* (2006) Rob Goffee and Gareth Jones argue that there are two main reasons why people choose to follow leaders:

1. **Authenticity**. The leaders are genuine and honest, they admit mistakes and they act with integrity. Authenticity in leadership is deeply important. We know from what has happened in recent years in UK politics that the general public dislike the concept of leaders failing to keep to their own

rules, and that, eventually, the 'do as I say but not as I do' approach leads to a breakdown of trust between the leader and the led

2. **Expertise and credibility**. They have relevant expertise and credibility. They understand the work and its complexity. The people they lead believe that they know what they are doing. They usually make good, informed decisions

In this book, Brian demonstrates both of these aspects in abundance. His authenticity shines through on every page. He writes about his mistakes; he explains – in a refreshingly honest way – how at times the stresses of his leadership role had an impact on his physical and mental wellbeing. We read how Brian, over his long career in school leadership, has tried to be the best version of himself and about how he learned, over time, to be a better leader. But he also demonstrates deep leadership expertise and gives good practical down-to-earth advice about the real problems that school leaders face. Leading schools is a complex, multi-layered and challenging process. What makes this book so impressive is that on every page it is clear that the author is someone who really understands schools and school leadership; someone who has lived and breathed it and, indeed, is still doing so. As we progress through chapters on wellbeing, inclusion, finance and leading teams as well as on managing change and working in challenging circumstances, the reader is given honest, no-nonsense perspectives on the lessons Brian has learned over his 19 years as a head teacher.

As leaders, we are all on an improvement journey. We learn, as Brian has done, from experience; from trying something out, reflecting upon it and trying to do it better next time. This usually takes years, indeed it takes a whole career. But if we are willing to ask for help, to seek out advice from those who have gone before us and to welcome challenge, we can speed up the leadership development process and learn more rapidly. If you are already a head teacher or aspire to be one, one of the ways to speed up that development process would be to read this excellent book.

Steve Munby

Reference

Goffee, R. and Jones, G. (2006) *Why Should Anyone Be Led by You? What It Takes to Be an Authentic Leader*, Boston, MA: Harvard Business Review Press.

Introduction

I have been a head teacher for what feels like a very long time, 19 years and counting. During this time, the role of the school leader has changed dramatically and I believe that we now face more challenges and accountability in the role than at any other time. This book looks to explore many of the big issues we face as school leaders and tries to make sense of how we find solutions while keeping our own wellbeing in check. As I have found, this is no small task.

I have led in schools across the South of England, in London, Bristol and currently the rural splendours of Somerset. When I take a moment to look back over my career (which is something we should all do throughout our time in this profession), it is with warmth and a sense of pride that I have been lucky enough to do a job that has such purpose, significance and joy attached to it. I have led schools in Special Measures and schools that received an Outstanding Ofsted judgement. I have worked with incredible teams in times of crisis and celebration. I have watched my schools pick up national awards and national condemnation. No training programme provided me the skills or knowledge to be ready to deal with these past 19 years. Nothing prepared me for that chant that I still hear echoing down the corridors to this very day:

You don't know what you're doing ... you don't know what you're doing.

Imposter syndrome is strong within school leadership. I live with many guiding principles as a school leader and the first one is very simple to remember but sometimes feels impossible to get right. As a school leader you have to face up to the fact that there will be many occasions when you feel out of your depth; that you really do not know what to do next. No matter how much experience you gain there will always be this uneasy feeling on your periphery, a heavy darkness stirring in the pit of your stomach leading you to feel that at any given moment someone is going to tap you on the shoulder and when you turn round and stare into their blank expressionless face they will look right through you and whisper, 'You haven't got a clue, have you?'.

It's not all doom and gloom, and my tactic for getting others to lead in schools is not to scare 99% from what, I fervently believe, is the best job in the world.

I want to be straight from the start though – there is no perfect book or brilliant course that prepares you for the role of leading a school, because much of it is about understanding yourself and how you respond to pressure and people within the school environment. I have been careful in writing this book not to make it a handbook of charts and templates or academically researched and evidenced theories, because school leadership is a fluid process that has much to do with context, feeling and empathy. I wrote it as a practising head teacher, as lived experience. Too often, I see people advertise the perfect solution for school improvement that looks whizzy, but no more practical than the dog-eared notebook with scrawled thoughts and ideas in my desk drawer. One of my priorities in writing this book was to be pragmatic about the role, to simplify it but also to inspire the reader to reflect on their own context and understand what works for them.

Better the devil you know

No matter where you are in your career the challenges of school leadership are many and endless. There will be times of stress so thick, so toxic, you will need to stop and remind yourself to breathe. One of the greatest lessons I have learnt is knowing that I will get through it; that the crisis of the day, week or month will pass and I will have learnt valuable lessons along the way. Surviving it is about using the skills I have built up over the years in education, and beyond, and applying them to keep going. It is about developing our leader resilience. It is not as easy as it sounds. One of the reasons I decided to write this book while I was still a head teacher was that I wanted to be able to reflect during the writing process. I also wanted to challenge my own thinking about the 'what' and 'why' of the role I had in running a school. The more I have written the more I have understood that leading in a school is about reflection and knowing yourself better. It has been at times cathartic and at others uncomfortable. This is what I mean in the book's title, *Lessons from the Head's Office*. This book is about the many lessons I have learnt – sometimes planned, sometimes stumbled over. There are many experiences in this book that I do not want to repeat, but there have also been many lessons that have helped me stay true to the role I have as a school leader.

'Better the devil you know' is a great starting point on the road to leading a school: know your strengths and your weaknesses in equal measure and face up to them, head on. Currently, when I hear that chant 'You don't know what you're doing!', I usually have a smile on my face because it reminds me that I need to find out a way to solve a problem rather than nurture my anxiety about it. This fear of being found out as a great pretender is something many school leaders I have met over the years struggle to manage; that they are expected to have all the answers and lead on every problem. Being at peace with this is a huge step in meeting one of the most important goals a school leader should have in their career: longevity.

Longevity

It is not awards or condemnation, fleeting moments of success or failure that will define our career – it is being able to look back and feel that what we did was fulfilling, worthwhile and effective. During the years, I have seen so many promising and talented teachers and school leaders stumble over the steps to the head's office – individuals ready for headship but for reasons unforeseen at the beginning unable to last more than a few years in the role. It is rarely through a monumental mistake (though they do happen). It is often through a combination of stresses and strains that slowly build up and make the possible seem impossible. It is a grinding down of resolve, confidence and influence, which highlights our mistakes and often fuels further bad judgement calls or inconsistent actions. It can be a horrible spectacle to watch from afar, emotive and personal. In some cases, it has even cost those leaders their livelihoods or lives. It is devastating for those who go through it and for their families. Once you go down the school leader route, once you sit in the leader's chair, it is very hard to walk away, to go back; therefore understanding this is a vital early step you must take. Do you know what you are accepting when you say 'Yes' to the job? I have had this conversation with aspiring leaders so many times. A job offer in headship is a great moment in the career of someone who aims to be a school leader; the problem is that until you try it you will never fully understand how you will cope with it because no other job in education places the full accountability of running a school so firmly upon your shoulders.

The reason I am still rambling the corridors of education is because I do not ignore that muffled voice reminding me 'I don't know what to do' as I creep past the staffroom door; I never shy away from not knowing what to do because these are often the most important things a school leader has to know about. I once had a mentor who said, 'If you can't sleep because school is still in your head, have a pen and pad at the bedside. Write down what is keeping you awake. It's very likely that you will be writing your School Development Plan'.

Once upon a time, the position of headmaster or headmistress seemed a fairly straightforward role. They were the foundations of the school, the discipline and authority. There was an element of mystery to what they did and no one would dare question them on it. Much has changed because expectations and accountability in the education system have changed. Expectations of school leaders have never been so high … When I was an acting head teacher in 2003 nothing fazed me, I was like a moth to a light and tackled every problem, big and small, with the energy of a thousand suns. I was relentless and most likely a nightmare for those who had to work alongside me. I made many mistakes and learnt many difficult lessons in those early years. Alongside constantly reflecting on my strengths and weaknesses I do my best to not make the same mistake twice, although as you will read in this book that is not always easy.

As I said, I often look back on my career to those days (even very recently) when I felt utterly spent and used, a husk of the perceived self I wanted to project. Over the years I have faced many challenges. I have been verbally and physically assaulted and I have lost count of the times I have been in meetings where I wanted to be anywhere else. A parent once shouted down the phone that I was complicit in 'attempted murder'; I remember hearing her partner, who was driving at the time, shout, 'What!?!'. And as he tried to grab the phone to apologise all I could hear were the screeching brakes of their car they were in. As a head teacher, you are the central point to so many people and often this puts you right in the eye of the storm.

I remember another time when a police officer started a child protection conference with, 'It's best we remove the glass … '. I remember thinking: why am I going to be sitting in a room with someone so volatile that the police were worried they may attack someone with a drinking glass? I am OK with this now because I have had to learn to be OK even when it makes me sad or scared, but for anyone who sees their future in school leadership you must understand that it comes with a cost.

A mentor once told me: 'Remember you have to treat everyone as though they have the wings of butterflies … and face the fact that they think you have the hide of a rhino.'

If not you, then who?

My hide is criss-crossed with scars, some deeper than others. They all leave their mark. When I was working in Tower Hamlets, a friend used to joke that I was on the front line of battle. Of course, it was nothing like this but there were days when I felt deeply troubled by my responsibilities, the events that unfolded and the complicated lives I was suddenly caught up in. I look back at my time there with rose-tinted glasses. It was the time of my life. Even as I write this I remember events so clearly: how I felt, what I said, where I was when certain things happened; the meetings where things were disclosed and handed over for you to sort out that were beyond any training. Like many of you reading this I became the school leader because I was a good teacher who took on more and more responsibility when the opportunity presented itself. Once I became a head teacher though, nothing prepared me for many of the situations I found myself in. Years on and I still get that sinking feeling, I still feel moments of anxiety, I still dread confrontation. I have just learnt to deal with these feelings. That's not to say they go away or stop having an impact on my wellbeing.

Rape disclosures, female genital mutilation, human trafficking, the sudden death of a parent or child, suicide, domestic abuse, divorce, the 7/7 bombings, staff disciplinaries, school failure (via SATs, Ofsted or feuding governors), a letter from a lawyer, a tribunal, parental complaints about almost anything you can imagine, 999 emergencies and a host of situations that make it seem like you really are in a war zone and not a school have all happened to me over the years. When you are faced with these awful things you will question whether it is worth the stresses. You will want to run, shout, hide or quit. This is only natural; it is the human in you processing the situation you find yourself in and of course, you want to run or react. The problem for many school leaders though is they feel they cannot run, hide or quit – that they are trapped in this world. I have always held on though, and yes – it has been worth it because I know I have always tried to do the best I could in the circumstances. In this book, I will talk a lot about how to handle your own wellbeing when faced with the many challenges the role creates. There is no clever trick, but there are some tests you must put yourself through to know how you are coping (or not) and what to do about it.

Even though there are dark times as a school leader, I would do nothing else. I am proud, blessed even, to be called a school leader. I have sat in my car on more occasions than I can count and sang at the top of my lungs bathed in the glory of being *The Head Teacher*. However, ignore the stress, try to hide from the hard-edged challenges of school leadership, at your peril.

I have learnt to deal with the trials and tribulations of school leadership because I have had to. I knew no other way as I stumbled from point to point. I learnt from head teachers with hardened hearts and a force field around them that twisted light away. I learnt from emotional wrecks – leaders storming out of staff meetings because someone questioned the font on the teaching and learning policy or was not paying full attention. I learnt from the many casualties of leadership I have witnessed over the years as much as the successes, each one a reminder that this is not a job for the insecure. Most importantly, I learnt from myself. I learnt how to reflect on the mistakes I made without allowing them to consume and destroy me. I learnt to stop worrying at night and working at weekends, and to appreciate the support I have around me.

I do not have a hard shell, or force field. I am not your typical roughly chiselled leader, chewing gum and spitting into the staffroom sawdust. My strength comes from my honesty and curiosity. I liken myself to putty. You can prod and twist me and I will change shape. You can sometimes see the marks you left but you will also see how I have changed. Whereas the school leaders with a hard shell? You can prod them repeatedly and you will see nothing, not a mark. Nevertheless, eventually a tiny crack appears, and sometimes slowly, sometimes in an instant, the crack grows and they begin to fall apart, to shatter before your eyes. Putting the shattered remains of a head back together is an almost impossible task. It does not end well. Yet the reshaped putty just looks different; maybe a little grubbier around the edges, but it has adapted to its new shape. A lot of what we do in leadership is about adapting to the best ways in which to get systems, run by people, to work. Making the system change for you rather than change for its purpose is usually one of the first leadership mistakes I see when supporting a school in difficulties. This is because all too often school leaders lead as though everything is about them.

I love the TV series *The Sopranos*, and sometimes, for a variety of reasons, liken leading a school to the paranoid loneliness suffered by Tony Soprano, the mob boss played by the actor James Gandolfini. I have met many school leaders over the years who have displayed more than a passing resemblance to the gangster, but it is the role he held within the mob that reminds me of school leadership. There have been a number of what I term 'antihero school leaders' growing out of the multimedia age, where your views can be put on trial by keyboard warriors who have very different ideas about what education should be. Therefore, if you are different then there's likely to be a group somewhere ready to tell you why you are wrong. Even when your approaches clearly work that will not be enough for some to stop their judgement, usually people who have either retired from a school or never actually led a school. This judgement from afar when you are the leader can overwhelm you or leave you under pressure and feeling vulnerable. It is another of the fine balancing acts a school leader needs to learn – how to overcome the fears of being unpopular and alone in the final decision. Therefore, a big part of leadership is learning not to be too precious about what other people think about your ideas or approaches. If they work in your context then be proud of that.

Nearly every head teacher and school leader I meet wants to do the right thing – morally in the right and leading with wisdom and compassion. No one wants to be a Tony Soprano for obvious reasons, but that does not mean we do not suffer the dark nights of the soul. The reality is that when you make a decision for your organisation someone, somewhere, is not going to like it or agree with it. Someone, somewhere, will feel they have a better idea (they often do) or they will be worse off because of the decision (sometimes they will). Therefore, many head teachers struggle with their leader-identity when making tough calls. They confuse who they are with who they (or others) think they should be and this in turn means they make one of the biggest mistakes we can make in our profession – we stop being authentic.

Diplomatic relations

I am fascinated by just how comfortable head teachers and school leaders are within themselves and how they want to be seen as the leader. I often find that as head teachers we are far from comfortable being our true selves. Staying true to ourselves is vital in leading a school, but we have to develop a flexibility within our own systems and that is often at odds with other people's perception of what they think we should be. We have to make decisions we do not want to make, say things we do not fully believe and behave in ways that are different from how we feel. We have to do this and still feel authentic, which is never easy. How do we adapt this system without seeming to not care about teacher wellbeing? Or understand the pressures our teachers face? First, we must acknowledge that it is not 'all about *me*'; that we work in teams and we need to empower them if we want that team to be functional and effective. Therefore, we have to become skilled at brokering compromise, influencing others, inspiring them to action – we have to learn to be The Diplomat. If you are a control freak, then being a head teacher is a mighty challenge, but also if you are not assertive enough then others will lose faith in your vision and your ability to lead. Once again, we are balancing many skills while holding true to ourselves. I have realised that there is a very fine line between being a good or bad leader. We should not be judging ourselves on one good or bad decision though. The key is in seeing what we do in the longer term and over time and being as comfortable in the small victories as much as the larger ones. This means for many of us starting out that we need to develop our patience rather than rushing head long in to change.

You had better believe it

When I became the acting head teacher, in dramatic fashion, of a junior school just off Brick Lane, Tower Hamlets (where I had been the deputy head for less than a year), I had ten minutes to talk to the departing head teacher and then we did not speak again for more than a year. Four weeks into my first headship, like so many new head teachers, I was given a mentor – an ex-head teacher who seemed almost cut from marble and scared me a little. I was excited though, as you often are when promoted, but also left with a rising sense of fear – much like passing your driving test and going out onto the road alone and staring down the slip road onto the motorway. When I met people for the first time in this new role I would introduce myself:

Hi, I'm Brian … em, I'm the acting head … well I'm the deputy but I've been promoted, for now anyway. So, how can I help you?

The first thing my mentor made me do was stand in front of her and introduce myself:

Hello, I'm Mr Walton. I am the head teacher.

She kept making me say it repeatedly until she said that she believed me. She even made me go home and practise it in front of the mirror. She told me, 'Once you stand up to do this role there is no pretending, there is no acting. You *are* the head teacher and you lead the school, so, *you* had better believe it'. I still do this from time to time, especially when doubt sets in. I stand in front of the mirror and say, 'Hello, I am Brian Walton. The head teacher'.

Throughout this book, I have set out the many different aspects that we need to consider as The School Leader. Alongside them, I have explained many of my guiding principles – simple rules that help me make sense as I navigate over the rough seas of headship when I feel lost or face challenges that seem overwhelming. I often look back to myself starting out in headship and think: What would I tell that version of *Brian*? It often helps, even after many years doing the role.

- Do it. It is a job which makes a real difference to the lives of others. It is never boring
- You will likely be scared – this is natural and nothing to fear
- You do not know it all. Furthermore, you never will. So seek out those who can help you
- Not knowing what you are doing is usually the first step in finding out what you need to do. Therefore, embrace it, do not hide away from it
- It is OK to feel emotional when overwhelmed – just not in front of children, parents, staff or Ofsted please
- Sometimes you will fail, sometimes privately and sometimes *very* publicly. Know that these failures will pass and learn the lessons they teach us
- You do not have to carry it all alone. Once you become the school leader you will find out there are thousands of others who know how you feel. There are many tribes of leaders all waiting to offer advice and the firm hand of assistance. The hard thing is making sense of it all within your own context
- You are no longer a teacher, as much as teachers often want you to be one. You do not teach all day and every day, mark books and track those individuals as you did when you were in the classroom. Do not confuse monitoring, observation and strategy with what they do.

Accept that with every passing term this skill set will slightly wither but like riding a bike you won't forget and you will be developing new knowledge and skills – but class-based teaching will become a skill unpractised. Therefore, do not be afraid to recognise this. I think many head teachers who say they are still good teachers do a disservice to the teacher role. Teaching is not something you dabble in, it is a practised daily craft and profession that is an art to be honed. That is not to say that head teachers should not know what great teaching and learning is – they should, but from their perspective. 'Head teacher' is a misleading title in the modern world of school leadership. That is why I often refer to the title 'school leader' throughout this book

- Take wellbeing very seriously. Do not roll your eyes at the mention of the word. That is the folly of the least experienced – or the heartless

- You may find that you can no longer do the job. Getting out is hard but to keep going is usually even harder. When things go wrong, do you have people around you who understand how you are feeling and what you are going through? Failing in the ultra-accountable education system can be harsh. Look around you and think about those who congratulate you and slap you on the back in the good times. Will they be there to hold you up in times of struggle? I will give you ten seconds to work that one out

Lessons from the Head's Office sets out the many aspects of school leadership I have come across in my career. It is far from comprehensive but based on the issues I still find that I am facing today as a practising school leader. As I hope you will see, it will be an honest and at times brutal look at the challenges. I believe that it is through learning from our mistakes and the many tests we face that we learn to do our best work. Being out of our depth is a fact of life for school leaders. What is important is that we learn to not fear our mistakes; that we learn to take control of them and become curious and analytical. It is how we respond to the pitfalls and setbacks that running a school creates that shapes us as leaders, and this is often the difference between success and failure.

1
On Leadershit

This chapter will explore the idea of 'leadershit' and what it means to the school leader. It will cover the following topics:

- What leadershit is and why it can be so destructive
- How to deal with leadershit while managing your time and energy
- Understanding the school year formula and your school context in order to plan ahead and prioritise critical times where leadershit can be at its most challenging and destructive
- Understanding what is important in the context of your school and priorities

Introduction

Being an effective school leader can be challenging even at the best of times. The problem is that there are many distractions and obstacles that can make the job even harder. Many of these are things that stop you doing the important strategic stuff and can pull you into a cycle of distraction, false challenge and time wasting. I like to call this stuff *leadershit*.

Leadershit can be:

- Any system that creates more work than is necessary
- Low-level, malicious or vexatious complaints
- Negativity about systems that work but aren't liked
- Governors who can't tell the difference between their strategic role and your operational duties
- Broad initiatives that don't take school context into consideration
- Views about your leadership from people who do not have the accountability of leading your school
- Pretty much anything that starts with 'Ofsted wants …'

The job of the school leader is to know what and where the leadershit is and learn to step over it.

The national head teacher standards for England and Wales clearly set out what leaders must do:

- Leaders must be able to uphold high standards of principled and professional conduct
- Establish and oversee systems, processes and polices that enable the school to operate effectively and efficiently
- Make use of effective and proportional processes of education to identify and analyse complex and persistent problems and barriers which limit school effectiveness, and identify priority areas for improvement
- Ensure the school effectively and efficiently operates within the required regulatory framework and meets all statutory duties

(Department for Education (DfE), 2020)

The key words within the standards are 'effective', 'efficient' and 'priority'. To lead well, we need to make an impact on the bigger issues within our schools and those three words are at the crux of what we need to be and do. This is so we can ensure high-quality teaching and achievement and make the education experience a positive one that changes the lives of children in our school community.

Many years ago I was planning a talk on 'authentic leadership' with my colleague and fellow head teacher Tim Browse. This later became a keynote speech for the popular annual PrimaryRocks conference, which grew out of the vibrant educational Twitter community. As experienced head teachers we wanted to share our understanding of the role leaders play in creating systems and processes for helping teachers and staff to do their job well and why this was critical in ensuring a high-quality school. We also wanted to share how challenging the barriers to being a good leader could be and how this could often impact schools through mundane and miniscule issues side-tracking the leader and creating problems of mythic proportions when in reality they didn't really matter. We wanted to show how easy it was to lose sight of what mattered in a school, so we came up with the term 'leadershit'.

What is leadershit?

Leadershit is the distractions and nonsense that get in your way and stop you doing the job you want and need to do. It is the systems – your own, countywide or national – that stop you being effective in your role. It can also be the views and opinions of others that challenge or sabotage the work you are trying to do to improve your school community. Much of this 'stuff' is not apparent until you become 'the leader'. Although teachers deal with leadershit all the time, it is only when you take on the additional responsibilities of leading that you realise just how much leadershit there really is out there. It is everywhere, and you will rarely go through a week without coming into contact with it on at least one occasion.

I want to be clear that it is not about *leader shits* – bad leaders; dictators of the staffroom or psychopathic head teachers hell-bent on making everyone's lives miserable. Leadershit in the hands of these people can be very destructive and often on an epic scale. I have worked with many school leaders who let leadershit distract them from their core purpose:

- Visionary leaders who completely changed direction at the slightest sign of challenge or mumbled concern
- Compassionate leaders who made concessions so others could meet their vision and then changed their mind, often creating confusion or favouritism
- Creative leaders who offered to take you on a journey but then left you stranded with nowhere else to go when they got bored with the details and wanted to focus on another project

All of them had vision for their schools, but when they got bogged down in the leadershit they were derailed and distracted. They lost that particular vision and with it they lost their direction, and this usually impacted the quality of their leadership and therefore filtered down and impacted on everyone else.

Leadershit is the stuff that drags your day or ideas into an unstoppable loop of pointless and time-consuming management. This, in itself, is destructive, but leadershit has an added tier of challenge for the school leader: it makes them feel powerless, useless or vulnerable.

After one newspaper interview, the local social media forum put up an article about it; all the comments were about how poorly my tie was knotted and how scruffy my hair was. I remember being really upset and knocked back by these comments; I spent days going on about them when I could have been doing something more constructive. The article was about me becoming a national leader, but rather than being proud about the accomplishment I only focused on the negative comments. This is a perfect illustration of the impact of leadershit. By this time in my career I should have been able to deal with stupid, petty stuff such as this and yet I spent hours moaning to everyone about how unfairly I had been treated. Leadershit can do this to you.

Leadershit is rarely about your strategy for leading a school, but about the worst of managing views, people, systems, processes and day-to-day administration, that gets in the way of your vision and effective leadership. It quite often comes in the form of an email and is almost always (though not exclusively) a statutory duty, a concern or a complaint about something in your school, including (and these are all real examples I have come across):

- Emails complaining about pretty much *anything*, including why Johnny is in a class with Billy, why Sarah is NOT in a class with Clara, why are the carrots purple, why is there a supply teacher, why don't children learn to sew, why didn't Mr Brown smile at me this morning, why can't my child dye their hair green ... Honestly, I could write a chapter just listing emails of this nature
- Facebook rants about anything, ranging from vaccinations, Brexit, parking, sanctioned bullying, sex or religious education, to staff leaving or getting pregnant or why the school banned sugary drinks
- Meaningless meetings about pointless things that have no real impact on children's learning outcomes or your leadership priorities – these are often sold to schools through innovation or consultancy; sometimes these meetings can be important, but are often too long where nothing productive is agreed upon. Even in the Microsoft Teams era, I see little change in pointless meetings, especially if they are longer than 45 minutes. Meetings can be prime leadershit
- Fifty-page documents on asbestos, policies that take hours to write which no one ever reads, biometric information, instruments of governance or data protection (even when important they can still reek of leadershit and drag you into the vortex of pointless distraction)

- The reproduction of data into another format for someone to read because they say they don't understand the original data
- A hundred-page, five-year School Development Plan laying out your journey to 'world class'
- Three years or longer budget planning
- Pretty much every Department for Education (DfE) email or piece of paperwork you need to complete to justify your budget under the fear that if you do not do it they will take money away from your school
- Being told what 'Ofsted wants' by people who have never run or set foot in a school and do not have to face Ofsted across the table

Leadershit is the nemesis of the school leader, and if you do not see it coming, if you are unable to get through it, then you can soon find yourself neck deep. Drowning in leadershit is not a good way to go. Often when people talk about the stress of leading a school they talk about the big stuff such as making cuts in a budget or a disciplinary hearing, equally it can be a smaller issue about something relatively unimportant that we did not expect that does the most damage. One of its most destructive elements is that it directs your focus from the important things you need to do in your school. Therefore, always remember:

> If you are under pressure, go for the priorities first. If you are **not** under pressure, go for the priorities first. You'll know what those priorities are because they will be either in your Development Plan, or an uneasy feeling in the pit of your stomach. If you cannot see any priorities, then it is unlikely you are looking hard enough and might need to wipe some leadershit from your eyes. If you really do not have any priorities then you are in the very rare and lucky position of being able to plan for the future. This is a rare and precious time for the school leader.

Leadershit is presented as *important* and *urgent*, especially by the person delivering it to you, but once you get to understand it you quickly realise it is nothing more than a waste of everyone's time, including theirs. The problem is that you cannot ignore it. Learning to deal with it, quickly and effectively, is a vital survival tactic for any school leader.

Time waits for no one

Dealing with leadershit is about knowing where you are spending your time and energy and having the courage to stop what you are doing if it is not making a positive difference to your school. The problem with leadershit is it makes you doubt yourself and eats away at your confidence, and this often ends up with you wasting time in the wrong places.

One of my observations of head teachers I have worked with is how they use their time. Quite often I'll be told 'I am overloaded', but then when we sit down and go through the 'overload' there are two or three things we all agree are just not priorities for anyone and staying late focusing on them is not impacting upon the challenges that matter. The leader is working to breaking point and those 'little' things can often be the straw that breaks the camel's back. This is usually because the leader has an unrealistic understanding of what others expect from them – this is sometimes imagined but can also be real. Therefore, they try to get on top of everything and end up not being able to focus on the things that really do matter, and these can then creep up on them and become overwhelming. It has always shocked me how easily this cycle can appear and how hard it is to break.

So I ask myself and others: 'What are you doing today that really matters?' How easily can you list the top three things that you must do? I usually stop at one or two; I write them down and never take them for granted. I do not use a special format for writing them down. At the start of most days (with a cup of coffee) I just open my hardback, plain paper A4 book and review the previous day's list, write down what I have to do that day and make it my mission not to leave work until I am happy I have done them, or made significant progress on them. If I have to think too hard about what I need to be doing then I tend to see that as a positive and no longer feel any guilt about this. In the early years of my headship these rare times of not being able to think of something did scare me as I thought I was missing something important, or just not doing the job properly. I have learnt to really understand what needs to be done and by when and ensure that I absolutely focus on achieving that.

I once went to support a school to find that the head teacher was the person who counted the petty cash – daily. Piles of coins counted every day – this was not some drastic reaction to a deficit budget, but 30 minutes of mindful unpressurised bliss that had become a leadershit habit. This was a very long time ago but I often think about the work I am doing and liken it to counting pennies. Should I really be doing this? Or, am I doing this because I don't want to face the things I really need to be doing? There is nothing wrong in taking time away from tasks to focus on something else, such as doing the washing up in the staffroom – it is acknowledging that this is what you are doing and knowing that you need to get back to the priorities as soon as possible.

A fantastic governor once asked the following questions that made me realise that my approach to lists needed to be far more than simply writing a 'to do' list: "How do you manage the list? Are there ever items that felt important yesterday, but not today? How do you stop yourself writing an unrealistic list? How do you make sure your list is strategic and not just full of 'counting the pennies'? Do you ever add stuff to the list that is just focussed on you and your wellbeing?" The answers to these questions were simple. I find that how I make lists evolves each year. It has to work for you and your context, and both change.

Know the academic formula

The school year is pretty formulaic and therefore we usually know a lot of information before September comes.

We have a lot of intelligence about when the pressure points of the school year will be:

- Christmas and end-of-year performances
- Lesson and work moderations as well as performance management
- Your staff, governor and senior team meetings are usually set out for the year
- Examinations, assessment deadlines and reports to parents are pretty much at the same time every year
- We know the day for staff meetings and we know when your INSET (In Service Training) days are

Having the certainties planned into the diary means that a school leader has an element of control over workload pressures, and alongside their senior leadership team they can organise time and balance out conflicting pressures as much as possible, or create support structures for when there are critical stress points within the year. We should know when we are busier than usual and plan to take this into consideration. Don't set a deadline for a research project on the same week you have five nights of performances to speak at. Don't set a critical staff meeting training session on the same week as data deadlines. I always sit down with my senior leadership team at the start of the academic year and plot out everything we already know about the year ahead. We then look at crunch points and rearrange things as soon as we can.

Swallowing toads

What are hard to plot are the things we 'enjoy' doing that can smother our time and the things that we find most difficult that we want to ignore. If we are not careful we can find ourselves planning for and doing what we love, which has little impact, and avoiding the important things we must do, which can have grave consequences. For example, having that difficult conversation with a member of staff is never easy and we can find ways of pushing it to one side, whereas telling a parent how well their child is doing is something every school leader looks forward to and enjoys.

I worked with a mentor early in my first headship who told me, in great detail, that I had to start the day swallowing a toad. The very thought still makes me shudder – which is the purpose of the statement. What she basically meant was that I had to get the unpleasant stuff out of the way first thing rather than spend the day worrying about it. Leadershit can sometimes become a welcome distraction, especially when there are horrible things on the 'to do' list. To avoid sitting down and starting a difficult conversation I have found that through leadershit I can create a lesser problem but make it seem like it is more vital and pressing. Rather than swallow the toad I'll start on a grasshopper – it's still unpleasant but slightly easier to swallow. The problem with this approach is the toad does not go away, it is still there staring at us from our desk the next morning and it may have become a little larger.

I have always sworn by the Eisenhower Matrix (see Figure 1.1 below). I have adapted it so that I no longer write down 'not important' or 'not urgent' because they are just that and I am wasting time writing them down. However, you can write them down as a way of noticing elements of leadershit. When I started using this grid I did use all four quadrants and was shocked at how full, and easy it was to fill, the not important and not urgent boxes. The most important area to focus on is what is 'important' and 'urgent'. That head teacher's report deadline, HR meeting, safeguarding issue – you will not struggle to find important things to be doing. I have spent time defining what is 'important' and 'not important' and would recommend you and your team do the same. It is surprising how views on what is important in our school can differ within teams. The urgency is the defining issue in terms of order. Safeguarding and urgent trump almost any other issue in a school. The top left-hand box is the stuff that you should be doing in the 'now'.

I have found many different ways to deal with leadershit, and one of them is asking, 'Do I have any of it in the Important Urgent box?'. I find that there is less and less of it as the years go by, though I do still find that the leadershit pops up disguised as important and urgent; this is often because of other factors I haven't had time to digest (yuck!), and realise that it isn't as important as it thinks it is. It is at this point you need to ask, 'What happens if I choose to ignore this?'. I once thought that ignoring what I regarded to be important would bring a hoard of officials knocking at my door demanding my head or a stint in the leadership repentance stocks. I then found it easier dismissing other people's important issues to focus on the important issues I saw and heard about in my school. As I became better at this and my confidence in knowing what needed to be done grew, I began to pick out the issues within my own school that were dressed up as important or urgent but were just distractions from the things we really needed to do. When you are able to see through the leadershit and ignore it you can find ways to be far more productive as a school leader. You also suddenly realise you have the confidence to be braver in your decision making because you feel more informed. A conversation with a governor put this much more clearly:

- identifying leadershit is a learnt skill and you have to practise to get good at it;

- you need to develop the ability to look at issues in the context of your school before you decide if they are important or urgent;

- eventually you'll develop an instinctive confidence in your judgement because you will feel well informed.

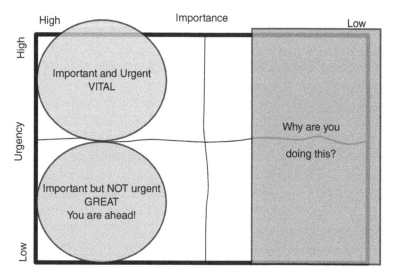

Figure 1.1   The Eisenhower Matrix

I got 99 problems – but Ofsted ain't one

Leadershit is usually the things of little value that smother our time and focus but there will always be things to do and worry about as a school leader. Understanding which ones to ignore and which ones to focus on is a vital part of successful school leadership. There is a real danger that some problems can take over your time and energy and when you analyse them you realise that they did nothing of real value for your leadership or your school community. In fact, you will often find they did nothing but damage to both. One way of identifying leadershit is through asking, 'Who does it belong to and what might their motive be?'. If you are dealing with a fringe issue, someone's gripe or a personal agenda it is quite likely taking you away from your core purpose of leading the school community. It is leading you down their alley where, if you are not careful, you could become lost, or worse. This is often one of the hardest leadership conundrums we have to deal with. It is agenda driven, often personal and comes in the form of complaints and criticisms.

I have probably found emails from parents, usually on a Friday night at about 7pm, one of the hardest issues to deal with. They will likely start with 'For whom it may concern' or 'Dear Gitface' and they can rant on and on for a very long time. The first lesson I had to learn was to not read emails on a Friday night, or any night. I then learnt to ensure that emails couldn't be directed to me by parents and then I learnt that I needed to make sure that someone from the office didn't helpfully forward them to me over the weekend or during the night. Once I took the initial shock factor of an angry social media post or email away, which usually escalated the issue and created a trail of emails that developed new even more complex problems, eight times out of ten I have found that parents are a lot calmer after the initial anger of the composition than if I had engaged with them during the weekend via email. One thing I have found time and time again is that meeting people face to face to resolve issues is almost always better than communicating through letters or emails. There is a lot to be said about how body language can be lost in translation and twist meaning out of all context. Starting a face-to-face meeting with 'How can I help?' and listening carefully as someone explains their concerns can take the sting out of any keyboard warrior. I tend to write as parents speak and work out what the core issues are. I often then ask, 'What would you like me to do?' Of course, this does not always work, but in most cases, I find that it does.

Another method I find useful to help me focus on the tasks that need doing is simple listing. I worked with a brilliant deputy (who is a very successful executive head now) many years ago who got me doing this. I find it works better if you list what you want to achieve on any given day, and this tends to have smaller issues included rather than longer-term priorities. Keeping focused on the *now* means you can make sure you are keeping on top of things. The benefit of listing easy-to-achieve things is the satisfaction you get when you cross them off your list. When you struggle to list actions for the day ahead then you can start to think about the *important* and *not urgent* list; you can start planning ahead. Of course, the very nature of school leadership means that situations can change very quickly, but those moments of planning ahead are useful, and lists work well for this. I have since developed this idea and have a whiteboard in my office with three columns: 'to do', 'in progress' and 'done'. Everything that needs to be 'done' on a strategic level over a term is initially written in red; other aspects are put on post-it notes. We usually do this during the first SLT (senior leadership team) meeting of the term, or through conversations I have with leaders at the end of term. Then, as things are completed, I rewrite them in black or I move the post-it notes across the board.

Rewriting feels good; moving post-it notes feels good. You also see which things are not moving or are staying red. It can be frustrating when things drag on and you have to rewrite actions from Term 1 in red into Term 2, but it does mean that you keep major priorities in focus and it allows you a strategic overview of the term.

Once a term is completed I take a photograph of the term and review the still-red writing (Are they still a priority?) and the black (Am I happy they are complete?). I then wipe the board down and rewrite the red I feel still needs to be completed alongside new priorities that might be term-specific or part of the School Development Plan. Once you have six terms of photographs it helps the coming year because some aspects will be regular priorities. As a final layer to this I create a Year Calendar with Key Dates and Events set out.

I mention School Development Plans because when we are dealing with priorities and keeping focused, a good way of knowing we are dealing with leadershit is when it is *not* on the School Development Plan.

Going with the Flow

Trying to work out the leadershit from the important parts of our role is not always easy. What is essential though is trying to find the balance in your role. Knowing when we are dealing with greater challenges or are bored by them are key skills we need to develop. Figure 1.2 is known as the Flow Model and I often visualise where the current list of things I need to complete come within this diagram. It is based on the work of the Hungarian-American psychologist Mihaly Csikszentmihalyi, who looked at the state of flow in what we do – when we are 'working happy' – and found that there were five key ingredients to this (Csikszentmihalyi, 1990):

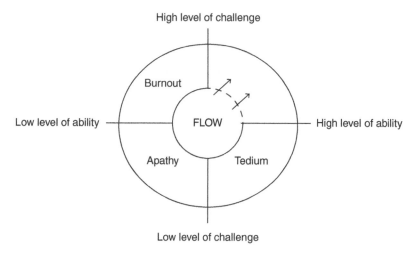

Figure 1.2   The Flow Model

- We were neither under-challenged nor over-challenged – our abilities and the intensity of the challenge were well met

Our work is often dictated to us by external factors we cannot control and therefore we need a good understanding of being over-challenged and how to cope with this. I explore this in more detail in Chapter 2, 'On Crisis Management'. Being under-challenged is also critical in this role and usually a good sign that someone is not focused on the core duties within their role. I have felt that in the past I may have become bogged down in leadershit simply because I had let it take over because I was under-challenged.

- There was a clear objective

A clear objective is critical for outcome-based leading. School leadership is a job where we can easily go home every night and feel we have got a brand new list of things to do, therefore we must set objectives that we can complete within the bigger picture. Time-specific objectives are easy for some aspects of the role – for example, the head teacher's report for a governor meeting is due on a specific date – but less so for bigger objectives such as 'improve teaching and learning'. Understanding the objectives that we set and breaking them down, spending time on them and seeing them in stages is an important part of setting clear targets. This is why when we write a School Development Plan we need to have spent time understanding what we are trying to do and why. I believe I am writing clear objectives all the time; it is not until I ask someone else on the team to explain what it means that I realise it is only me who thinks it is clear.

- We were getting constant feedback around the progress of the task

Gatekeeping projects is a critical mistake a school leader can make. Sharing our projects at all stages – not just when they become complex or difficult – and taking people along with us means we can constantly feel that we are not alone in trying to complete a project. We have to balance this with an understanding that everyone is busy and they don't want to constantly hear about updates, but sharing progress and being open to questions at the right time allows for a sense of ownership and progress. The best way to do this is to ask the teams we work with.

- The task was of our own choosing – we had ownership of it

This is not always possible, but understanding our team strengths and not taking on tasks that we don't have the time, knowledge or skill to complete is a strong part of leading in a successful school. Empowering our teams and having the trust to hand over tasks (including the ones we really want to do) means that we focus on task completion rather than control of the task.

- We were intensely focused on it

The flow line is a vital area in which to put the task. This is when things are working at a good pace, with the right level of focus, good feedback and a deadline in sight to an outcome that was agreed. You are unlikely to have the luxury of solely concentrating on one task in a school – but you can take on a task and dedicate the right level of focus to it so that you complete it well. To do this you need a good understanding of everything you are dealing with (lists, Eisenhower Matrix and School Development Plan). Problems will arise when you take on too many tasks or you don't deal with the leadershit and suddenly you are overwhelmed.

Another vital factor as a school leader is how you are supporting your team through setting tasks that are not over complex and are a match for their skills, especially giving them time to feedback on progress and helping them when the task strays into over-challenging burnout or under-challenging boredom.

Conclusion: Practise what you preach

An important thing to remember about leadershit is that it never goes away. It is a constant and will be with you in your first and your last year as a school leader. In fact, it is not exclusive to leaders, it starts in the classroom. Teachers deal with this daily; distractions that stop them teaching, activities that get hijacked or parental pressure go hand in hand with the teaching role and can have a profound impact on effective teaching and learning. It is only as they gain experience that they learn to cope with it and find ways of avoiding it. Learning to carefully dodge the leadershit and the additional problems it brings is often about experience but it is also about our confidence and vision for how we want to operate.

Therefore, another task that I do a lot as a school leader is look at what I am asking my teachers to do. Am I creating unnecessary burdens and wrapping them up as important or urgent? This is such an important task because as far as I am concerned I have one duty when it comes to my teachers, and that is to *free them up to do their job*. As my fantastic governor said, "A head teacher that isn't dealing with their own leadershit is likely to create even more leadershit for their teachers and senior leaders to deal with. Leadershit is a positive feedback loop, left unchecked it breeds!". There are so many initiatives, directives, expectations, gadgets, gimmicks and demands out there that if you are not careful you can end up with your teachers doing anything *but teach*. At its heart, leadership is about understanding the core of our duties and translating this across the school. For example, when monitoring teaching and learning, rather than focus on the teaching, I often look at the systems and processes the leaders have created that impact on what the teacher is able to do – are they enabling the teacher, or are they a barrier? In the past it could have been expectations that *all* teachers were expected to meet regardless of context or the age of children in their class, or marking that had to be in a certain colour, or to follow explicit rules, or at least five spellings having to be corrected in every piece of work. When you step back and analyse this approach you realise that you can be the biggest problem in why a teacher is not as effective as they can be, that the lesson you are watching is constrained because you have created the barriers. So often those systems are not about teaching and learning but more to do with consistency and control – neither of which have all that much impact on children in particular classrooms learning more. A lesson observation that looks at what your teachers have to cope with regarding the leadership expectations can be an eye-opener. It is about going back to our core purpose regularly and reflecting on what we are doing that is making a real difference to the lives of those associated with our school community. It is about having a vision rather than reacting – trigger-like – to all that comes our way, and it is about being brave enough to change our systems to meet the needs of the teachers rather than the system itself.

I have been asked, 'Do you know where the key to the cleaner's cupboard is?' 'No'. And I have made it my leadership mission to never find out. From my perspective this is to make sure that I am a good, strategic leader, not someone who holds the keys to every door and knows every detail about the structure and history of the school. This is often legacy stuff and I want to lead by looking forward, not backwards. Eight years into my current headship and there are still doors I have not opened, and I want to keep it that way.

Leadership is about not getting lost in the leadershit. It is about knowing and being focused on the core priorities within your school. It is about creating the freedom and time to deal with what matters most.

References

Csikszentmihalyi, M. (1990) *Flow: The Psychology of Optimal Experience*. New York: Harper and Row.

Department for Education (DfE) (2020) Headteachers' standards 2020. Available at: www.gov.uk/government/publications/national-standards-of-excellence-for-headteachers [accessed 28.10.22].

2
On Crisis Management

This chapter will explore:

- How the school leader needs to be prepared for a range of crises – big and small
- The varied threats school leaders face and how they must learn to deal with them while managing their own wellbeing
- The wider impact they can have on the school community and individuals

I was in the toilet fighting back my emotions and hoping a member of staff would not walk in. I was fighting a losing battle as my feelings got the better of me. I was not embarrassed that the barrier had come down. In fact, I just felt a sense of relief.

There are times of crisis when leading a school will leave you feeling so overwhelmed you can sense the control over your feelings slip away – that composure you know you must show to others, lost for a moment in a sea of uncertainty and exposure that leaves you feeling naked and helpless. Watching the emotional turmoil of a school leader in public is a very uncomfortable thing, akin to watching your mother or father cry. Therefore, having control over our emotions in public is a very important part of ensuring we lead our schools with the confidence of others.

I looked at myself again, took a deep breath, carefully wiped my eyes, and stepped back out into the school corridor. I became the 'head teacher' again. It had been a private moment, alone in the toilet (sometimes a sanctuary for the school leader). It was not the first time I had felt so overwhelmed and I knew it would not be the last. As I walked down the wide corridors to the staffroom, I passed the school hall where my deputy was starting an unexpected whole school assembly. I could hear the distant sirens getting closer, coming down Vallance Road in Whitechapel, London, outside my school. I tried to word what I was about to tell the gathered staff but could not find the right words. As I entered the staffroom all eyes were immediately on me, as I knew they would be. They could sense that something was wrong, but I knew that what I was about to tell them would have massive implications. Telling your staff that the sirens they can hear speeding past your school were because a bomb has exploded at the tube station a few streets away, knowing that many of your staff would likely have loved ones travelling on the tube that morning, to school and work, is an awful thing to do. Even harder was keeping my emotions in check as I told them knowing that my wife and newborn child had a hospital appointment that morning and would also be on the underground, and despite trying I had been unable to contact them on my mobile phone. Even now, I do not remember much of what I said at that staff meeting and the rest of that day is still a hazy blur.

Introduction

I have felt as though I have been at breaking point many times during my career as a head teacher. This is especially true when a crisis arises alongside other challenges, professional or personal. There are countless issues that can play on the mind of the school leader when alone in their office at night, and a crisis can often be a very unwelcome bedfellow pushing our resolve, skills, knowledge and wellbeing into unknown territories. However, having to face these challenges is the reality, and we need to be able to effectively understand and manage the trials and tribulations of leading a school alongside a variety of emergencies big and small. As I write this, I have spent a sleep-disturbed night worrying about a child at risk of permanent exclusion. If you add in a crisis alongside these everyday challenges, you can understand why many head teachers do not see out their full terms, struggle with stress, leave the profession or move on. There are times in headship when you feel like you are on the eve of a great battle where the odds of something terrible happening are inevitable, and fully stacked against you. It is an ominous feeling but one you need to become comfortable with. One of the most important factors you need to understand in any crisis is that people need to feel safe. This is not always about physical safety but deeper than that, they need security and clarity. It is the leader's job to provide this, and therefore we must control the crisis as best we can.

Living with the FONK

School leadership can produce many dilemmas that push the outer limits of our capability and resolve. Crisis management is a vital part of the school leader's skill set and we need to know and understand how we will react in a wide variety of situations where we are under sustained or sudden pressure. I have broken dealing with crisis management down into four distinct areas:

- Anticipation – predicting and preparing for a crisis
- Navigation – understanding the structure you need to follow in the event of a crisis
- Communication – knowing how you will communicate, often within a fast-moving or complex situation; as well as where you can get resources and help
- Reflection – learning from the experience

Sometimes, in a crisis, the focus of the pressure is obvious and time limited, such as a fire, and at other times, the crisis can drag on and grow in complexity and pressure. The coronavirus pandemic in 2020–21 created huge challenges within education in different ways at different times and has presented schools with unique and extraordinary challenges for many years to come. All of these situations need school leaders to be in control, assured and able to find solutions that help the community cope with the situation.

Thankfully, these types of crisis are not everyday occurrences, but when they do come, they often bring with them the Fear Of Not Knowing (the FONK). As a school leader, you will come face to face with situations in which you do not have immediate answers but in which everyone will either expect you to 'have a plan' or look to you for guidance and information. In some emergencies, the solution is easy. A fire alarm rings and we follow our procedures. We get everyone calmly and safely out of the building and follow the rehearsed systems. Afterwards we review the event to see if we need to make adjustments or changes to ensure we tighten any gaps or concerns. In other situations, the crisis can be sudden and unexpected, such as the death of a child, member of staff or parent, and we feel the situation overwhelm us with unknowns as we struggle with our own emotions.

And breathe ...

The first principle I review under any difficult challenge is: 'How am I feeling right now?'

This is based on some feedback I got very early into my first headship when a professional coach I was working with said 'Breathe Brian, breathe!', as I walked down the corridor to deal with a child who had got onto the school roof and was ripping up the lining and throwing it onto the playground. Placing yourself in the moment during a crisis does not take long and allows you to gauge how you feel and very importantly how you are presenting. I will often do the 7/11 breathing technique before walking in to deal with any crisis no matter how big or small. I consciously breathe in for 7 seconds and then breathe out for 11 seconds, two or three times. It just works for me and allows me to link back to myself. It is quick and easy but is my reminder to be in control. I think about it in the same way as a flight attendant safety briefing before a plane takes off and how you need to secure your own oxygen mask before assisting others. A big part of dealing with a crisis is how others observe you and interpret your actions. Therefore, seeming calm (when you are not) and being clear (when you feel anything but) are vital aspects of managing a crisis. Nothing says 'panic' more than someone struggling to breathe.

Anticipation: I predict a riot

I worked with an excellent chair of governors in my second headship who taught me much about how to lead a school, but we always clashed over one area that obsessed him. He wanted a detailed plan in the event of a plane crashing into the school grounds. I always struggled with this and would joke, 'If we do a Plane Plan can we also do a Meteorite one? What about Killer Clowns?'. There was an element of method in his thinking though. The school was on the edge of the flight path to a major airport. He was anticipating a worst-case scenario, and at this stage in my headship I just could not bring myself to imagine such a thing. He had been a head teacher himself and used to tell me about a school he ran in the middle of a city and how the signs that there would be a riot were there for years. In 1980 that riot happened, at which point the damage had been done and it was too late. His line was simple: 'Being prepared for it might not stop it, but it's better than being wise after the event.'

Anticipation is now a much bigger part of school life. We do risk assessments all the time and this is where we need to take the possibilities of events seriously. I rarely do a risk assessment alone and will often pay professionals, work with other head teachers or use model policies because it is not my area of expertise. However, I now recognise that taking time to think through what could happen, though a dark and depressing thing to do, is an important part of being a good school leader. I have thought through, no matter how unlikely, what I would do in the event of a terrorist attack, an angry stranger with a knife, or the death of someone on site. There are no risk assessments set up for these but there are procedures such as lockdown, communication lines and probable reactions that I have played through in my mind many times. This might seem a little fatalistic, like I am the kind of person who looks for fire exits when in a building (I am), but a critical aspect of leading is having an idea about what you would do in any given situation because doing something is very likely to be better than doing nothing (though not always). It is certainly not something you have to do very often because the likelihood is so small, and yet:

The bell for the end of the day sounded and children poured out of school. I was on the main gate saying goodbye when a parent told me that they had just seen someone stabbed on our road and the person who did it was on the loose. My senior team were also out and we immediately decided to get everyone we could back inside the school gates and close them. I remember standing there thinking, what will I do if the attacker comes this way? Minutes later two police cars sped up and asked that we keep everyone there. Twenty minutes later the police told us we could let everyone go. One parent still shouted at me on the way out and said I had made her late for her appointment.

I had imagined a scenario like this – a crisis at the end of the day when your normal controls were no longer fully effective. What happens when a crisis takes place at the most inconvenient time? I have always been one to set the fire alarm off during lunch, or a wet playtime. Making the decision to run into the road and ask people to come back into school was instinctive, but not the first time I had thought about it.

As leaders, it is our responsibility to be prepared for the worst, and it is through anticipating what could happen that we can gain some understanding about how we might react.

Stage 1: Forewarning

In some crises, you get a forewarning, maybe a letter threatening legal action or a meeting with a member of staff or parent that leaves you worried. If you do get this forewarning you can anticipate what could happen and prepare for it. It might not stop the crisis, but having time to think through, talk to others and prepare is very valuable. I tend to do a brief slimmed-down Strengths Weaknesses Opportunities and Threats (SWOT) analysis in my head at this stage.

- What strengths do we have to tackle the possible crisis? The people and resources that we could call on – colleagues with experience in this area, HR, your chair of governors.
- What weaknesses do we have within the team or structures that could make this problem even harder to tackle?

In truth I tend to skip over 'Opportunities', but when given time to reflect on any crisis you will find that they do exist (for example look at the development of online communication technology during the Covid-19 pandemic; I almost never have to travel half a day now to go to a meeting and the opportunities for good-quality training are so much better – and cheaper).

Threats: What will they actually be? Are these physical threats or legal ones? Knowing this can help to give us some understanding and preparation when the next stage comes into play.

Navigation: Walk the line

When a crisis arises, you can be in a situation where you need to act without a full grasp of the situation. Navigating through a crisis is about being able to monitor a volatile situation while trying to control it. It can be about how you get from one place of crisis to another place of safety.

There are a number of crisis scenarios in schools where policy and systems help. Fire drills are good at quickly and calmly getting everyone out of the building. Lockdowns are good at keeping everyone in their classroom, or being aware of a fast-changing situation. Having walkie-talkies is a good way of keeping staff in communication during an on-site crisis. We have about 60 at my current school. Training staff in first aid, ensuring the asbestos register is up to date (I once had an external IT company try to drill into walls with asbestos, but thankfully we stopped them before they began). These everyday or annual types of procedure are vital in creating a system that protects your school community and ensures that emergencies can be steered safely when they happen. Paying for a yearly health and safety report is vital money well spent.

There are many other types of crisis though that are less directional and harder to plan for. These might not have guidance or procedures attached to them. Let us look at some examples of these:

- A parent having a road accident outside the school and needing medical attention
- A child falling out of a tree in the park into the school grounds and having their thumb cut off by the metal fence railings
- A child breaking their kneecap, arm or leg and the ambulance taking hours to arrive
- A governor or parent committing suicide
- A parent fight at the end of the school day
- A member of staff shouting at you in a staff meeting and storming out
- A governor writing a vicious critique on your leadership and sending it to everyone at 3am
- The British National Party, or anti-vaxers leafleting outside your school
- A legal letter saying that someone who fell on your grounds (that you knew nothing about) is claiming for damages
- Flooding or fire that wrecks a classroom
- The last minute unpredictability of snow days (school leaders hate snow days!)
- A teacher quitting on the spot
- Outbreaks of notifiable diseases
- A member of staff breaking the law, or getting arrested
- Allegations of sexual misconduct
- Strike days

Yes, all of these have happened to me as a head teacher and I did not see most of them coming as I got out of bed on those days.

When we face a crisis there is, at times, a feeling of walking a tightrope. You know that you need to get across it without falling. The good thing is that tightropes always lead to a destination point; the bad thing is it's messy when we fall off. I try to visualise how I will navigate through any crisis.

Stage 2: Boom!

The moment the reality of the crisis fully reveals itself can be horrible. It may be a slow development to a point at which you know you are now facing *serious implications*, or it may be a sudden moment that needs immediate action. Regardless of how it develops, it can bring with it a number of strong emotions including fear and anger. It is where we cross the line from the fear of not knowing to the horrible reality of not knowing.

This is the point at which we breathe and steadily tell our brain that we are calm. Anxiety is contagious and leaders can be super spreaders. This is the point at which we begin to navigate our way forward in the spotlight. It is the tricky moment but we must remember that we need to ensure we feel that we are in control of as much of it as possible, including the delegation of tasks to others.

Communication – say the right thing

Communication is vital at all levels of school leadership and an integral part of life in education, and never more so than when dealing with a crisis. At this time, we need to be seen as calm and focused on helping everyone through the situation. This means we need to think carefully about our communication and the information we are sending. We also need to think about the timing of this information – too late or too early and we can end up sending confusing messages and then having to deal with further questions and clarifications. We also need to think about how clear the messages are. As I have practised this, I have learnt that ensuring the message is precise and short is often the best way. Three-page letters explaining a situation can often send a mixed message or leave a situation open to many other areas of enquiry. With a crisis it is best to say what has happened and what we are doing about it rather than trying to explain the situation in detail. That is something we will do in the next stage.

Repetition

The repetition of messages is very important, as it is easy to assume that because we have said it, everyone has understood it. This is something we should never take for granted. In a crisis, the repetition of our key message helps everyone understand what we are doing and how we are doing it. For example, give parents too much information and we could end up making the message too complicated, and have to field many more questions from them.

Simplifying the core message is crucial when we want everyone to take effective and timely action. Briefing your office reception staff is a good way of keeping the message focused.

Think like a hostage negotiator

When dealing with a crisis I believe there is much we can learn from the people who need to hold conversations under incredibly difficult circumstances, such as the police or Samaritans.

- How do we understand the concerns of those impacted by the crisis – on all sides?
- How do we take on board other people's strong emotions and help calm them?
- How do we speak calmly when our heart is beating fast?
- How do we find the right words and actions?
- How do we build trust quickly?

I often imagine what it would be like to be a hostage negotiator. That must be all about crisis management under massive pressure. Maybe I just like the idea of making my job a little bit sexier:

Receptionist: 'Mr Walton, we have a 347 Code Red Situation!'
Mr Walton: 'What! A parent is swearing on the playground? Right, where's my hi vis jacket?'

Un-social media

A very difficult and modern dilemma to manage as a school leader is social media and the things that can be written on it about you, your school or community. Whether in a public forum or brought to your attention via a parent's negative comments it can be at least hurtful and at worst responsible for escalating a crisis.

The problem with human beings is when we are insulted (or seemingly insulted) we feel the need to respond, to have our say and allow 'justice' to be done. I have learnt to think very carefully before I make any response on social media. When blind (ignorant of the facts), unfounded attacks can be made and put forward as though they are hard evidence of what 'everybody' thinks, it can be very hard to sit back and say nothing, though this may be the best course of action.

Social media is particularly effective when it comes to the short pithy attack where people think they are being clever or funny and what they write is consensus. Usually the worst posts are written anonymously by keyboard warriors who seem to be on a relentless crusade, but no one is invisible. It is usually not that hard to work out who wrote the post; quite often, someone will tell you. Unlike abusive phone calls or an angry meeting, social media attacks are for all to see, but this can help you more than you think, as I will explain in the principles I use when dealing with them, below.

Number 1

Never respond on that medium immediately and ensure that no one connected to your school does either. Social media posts can escalate very quickly and when you do respond you want it to be carefully thought through. By responding on social media you give that platform validation. If this is your normal practice, then that is OK. We have both a Facebook and Twitter account at my school. We respond as an organisation – but we have always thought through what we are going to say before we say it. We often just ignore the posts because a public response might make the issue develop in a way we cannot fully control. The best course of action in most crises is to talk directly to the people involved – face to face if possible.

Another issue to consider when responding to social media comments is that by responding we send out a message that it is 'OK to communicate your dissatisfactions via social media'. Schools have complaints procedures, and if someone has a complaint we need to be comfortable signposting this to them so that they can follow the proper procedures.

We often find that the best way to respond is from a school account that does not identify who is posting, signposting them to the school office e-mail or, if appropriate, to the school complaints policy. Do not be afraid of this process because it is there for this very reason.

Number 2

Do you need to respond? Really? If a handful of people are throwing statements around anonymously, writing a whole-school newsletter response because of what will turn out to be three or four people – who, no matter what you do, will never be satisfied – is not going to change that. But, if you feel the post has gained traction and you can clearly explain why it is wrong, then writing to your community might be the best way to address the issue directly.

Number 3

If it is bad enough to warrant a response, you may want to brief staff and governors (always keep your chair briefed). Check that it has not spread to other social media platforms. Prepare a letter home to parents, and assume that the press will be in touch very soon and plan the message you wish to give them. Preparing a press statement is a good way of summarising the status of the crisis. You want to have that in place before a journalist calls you for a statement. A press statement is also a good way of thinking through any crisis. I have a number of professionals I can call on in the event of a crisis who know what questions to ask and how to write a public statement (look up your local journalists or talk to them about freelance work). I would highly recommend getting to know who your local public relations expert is and giving them a call when you feel you could do with some grounded advice about handling the communication aspect of a crisis.

Number 4

Seek legal advice if the attack is particularly nasty (especially if people are named). You will be surprised just how much you can do. In some circumstances you will need to call the police as well. A legal letter gives you some level of assurance because it can bring clarity to the situation, but be careful because it can also bring additional tensions and prolong what may have been a storm in a tea cup.

Number 5

Think *big* picture. Remember the facts about what you do in your school. Do not lose sight of this because someone has said something that if they could see it rationally (or it was said against them in the context of their job) would shame them. I do think we have to have better protection within schools – especially when sections of the media can print all sorts of unfounded attacks on the teaching profession. School leadership puts individuals into many situations where they can be personally attacked for the decisions they make – sadly now a fact of school leadership and being a teacher – therefore we need to understand what we can do rather than feel helpless about it.

I think the hardest thing to deal with when you read horrible things about yourself or your school is how much it upsets you (even when you laugh it off). You are left thinking: Why would someone want to do this? What are their motives? What are they getting from this? These are deeper philosophical questions; the feeling of being valued is a vital part of mental wellbeing and also an intrinsic part of being a head teacher or school leader within a community. Being criticised for one of the thousands of things you have to do can consume you and cloud out all the other things you do, important things like ensuring a great educational future for the children attending your school. Within a crisis, it bites even deeper because you know that communication is a key part of dealing with the problem and social media reflects on you badly. At times like this look at your last school parent survey – remember the bigger picture and how a handful of unhappy people are not the majority view.

Reflect: Shine a light

I could smell the smoke before the fire alarm went off. We were in the middle of a massive new building project that was converting our open -plan school into classrooms. There had been fire alarms before but this time it was not a drill. The teachers and children clicked into fire drill mode and like a well-oiled machine, everyone was out, calmly and orderly in very good time. I felt proud.

The fire truck arrived in swift time and I walked confidently over to the people pouring out of it, noticing the small plume of smoke rising from the roof.

'Is everyone accounted for?'

'Registers are in and, yes, all the children are on the playground.'

'And all the adults?'

'…Ummm? I think so?' I looked around …

'You think so? I have to send my team in there and you THINK so?' He shouted this and everyone heard him. I just stared down at the playground in shame.

Review. Act. Review.

We all love when things go exactly as planned, but the reality is often nothing like the plan. We need to be able to keep our approaches under constant review so that we can adapt to different situations in the event of a crisis. It is through the review process that we can begin to see the different perspectives and how the crisis is affecting others. Only seeing it from our perspective is in itself a fault in our plan. Remember that your crisis is also very likely to be other people's crisis – sometimes it will be worse for them.

Stage 3: The aftermath

This is the point at which you can chalk a crisis down as 'experience'. It is the time to think how you coped with it. An important part of this process is to ask trusted people within your organisation how they thought you coped with it. If you are brave, ask the people you may not usually ask. Go outside your normal boundaries. All this feedback – though at times difficult to take, so do not overdo it – can help you understand how you came across to others leading through the crisis. This is important because if there are areas to work on you will need to think about this before the next inevitable crisis, big or small.

Black swans

The other question to think about now is:

Did we see this coming? What were the signs – if any?

The philosopher Bertrand Russell used the analogy of a chicken to explain something called the Black Swan principle in his 1912 book, *The Problem of Philosophy* – how a chicken fed by hand every day becomes used to humans and therefore comes to believe that they are no longer a threat. There is no evidence to suggest otherwise, therefore the chicken never sees the fact that it will be killed for meat coming.

The Black Swan principle is about predicting events that we have not foreseen, and was based on the idea that in the 15th century there were no reports of black swans and therefore it was assumed that all swans were white. When events we could not have foreseen happen, it is at this stage we can try to make sense of it all and work out whether the signs may have been there before but we just did not see them.

Being reflective after an event is not always comfortable and may uncover aspects of our practice that may make us cringe, but post-crisis analysis is a vital aspect of moving forward as a school leader – especially if you were in the driving seat. The benefits of hindsight do not always mean we will be able to see off future emergencies, but they usually mean we do not make the same mistakes again. In many situations in school leadership, this is an invaluable lesson.

Custodians of hope

Another practice I have developed over the years is to have drinks out with close head teacher friends. We all need to find our fellow colleagues and build a trusting friendship. After catching up about general things (TV, film, books, food and music) we always end up somewhere quiet and private to share our challenges and give an honest and often unsweetened response. It works for us and we tend to laugh through it. Sharing how you are coping with the difficulties you are facing as a leader with people who know and understand what you are talking about is vital. These have to be people you trust to give you their honest appraisal, no matter how hard this is and how much you do not want to hear it. It is important this is not your partner, nor a close friend not in school leadership. I feel it should be kept away from your more personal life because this can cloud judgements. Part of longevity within school leadership is being able to keep the rawest elements of your job firmly out of your personal life. Therefore, building your professional support network, from your days as a teacher and beyond, is a vital aspect in coping with any given crisis. Though my close group often give me unforgiving critical appraisal, deep down they are my custodians of hope because they are people I know I can trust and I often find they reflect the struggles I have and make me feel that I am not alone.

A murder of crows

This support cannot be underestimated, because most head teachers know that facing a 'murder of crows' alone is a truly terrifying prospect. I always look to my support network when the 'murder' assembles. In folklore one of the explanations for the collective noun ('a murder of crows') is that crows will gather and decide the capital fate of another crow. There is often very little you can do to stop a brewing crisis but there is a lot you can do to cope with it. Throughout my career, I have often been shocked at the number of brilliant colleagues I have worked with who leave the profession, sometimes of their own choosing and sometimes forced. I have spoken to many of them since and they have always described the pressures they felt and how that was the deciding factor.

In the following chapter I will explore wellbeing and how we make sure that it is one of the most important features within our leadership approach, because when we face the many challenges we have to ensure that we keep being well and keep others well – otherwise we cannot survive in the school leader role.

3
On Wellbeing

This chapter will cover a number of areas:

- Why managing our own wellbeing needs to be a priority task and how we need to constantly monitor it – even when things *seem* to be going well
- A look at the impact that the pressures and repercussions of the daily challenges a leader faces can have and the ways in which we need to reflect on and build our resilience without underestimating the fallout
- How we must learn from our experiences, no matter how painful, to develop our skills and knowledge and nurture the craft of school leadership

This chapter explores one of the most overused and misunderstood aspects of school leadership – being and feeling well within the role. What my many years as a school leader have taught me is you cannot underestimate the impact that school leadership has on wellbeing. It is a key factor in your success or failure within the role and therefore you must find ways to protect it at all costs.

Breaking heads

There are times when the school leader has to work under absurd and unrelenting pressures. This can come from a variety of directions, most commonly (though not exclusively) school finance, societal, human resources (especially staffing), child protection, Ofsted or complaints. None of these challenges are unusual when you are responsible for running a school. In fact, it could be argued that they are an inevitable aspect of school leadership and what we need to do is learn to effectively navigate our way through the challenges they bring while managing our own reactions to them. In particular I have seen more and more that societal issues are now very much part of the work a school does; social care, financial support, housing, domestic violence, cost of living and anxiety are issues that have become entwined into the daily organisation and operation of how schools work. At our heart we are teachers, and learning is our profession, but it is now almost impossible to do the role effectively without understanding and tackling the many challenges our communities face.

Therefore, school leaders need to understand the impact that leading a school can have on their wellbeing. We must lead well or we can become part of the problems our schools face. Quite often we look at problems as though they are isolated challenges to overcome. Invariably many of the problems are tangled into the complex narratives of our school, parents, staff and own lives and part of the problem is how we unpick them to deal with the core issues. It is very rare that we deal with the bigger problems in neat and tidy ways, ticking them off a list one by one. Many of the problems drag on, take strange turns, get worse, escalate or seem to go away – to then suddenly pop up in an email on a Friday night or a conversation in the corridor. Therefore, a huge factor in being able to lead and manage challenges is ensuring that we feel confident as the leader, that we are well in body and mind and able to take each challenge on without allowing it to overwhelm us. An important part of this is understanding our sense of place and belonging within the role we have as the school leader. My wellbeing has always suffered most when I have doubted this.

If we are not mindful of our own wellbeing, the pressures that we are under as school leaders can creep up on us and in turn have a huge negative impact on our health and therefore our ability to be effective and confident leaders.

When working at a school in Special Measures in 2013, I suddenly became impotent. It happened almost overnight and lasted throughout my time supporting the school and it took months to return to normal. I was a forty-something, healthy man who had run a half marathon and often cycled long distances. I was a good body weight and yet my body was shutting down on me. Initially I was shocked and thought that there was some terrible underlying disease or medical diagnosis waiting for me. After an hour with a consultant, they confidently established that I had *stress*. I was outraged. I felt like they had wasted my time. How could stress be a professional diagnosis? Surely it was just a fact of life?

Stress? What stress?

I believed that the consultant did not really know what they were talking about and initially wanted a second opinion. I told them that I 'loved my job' – I skipped in to the sound of music, sang at the top of my voice during the car journey home, laughed with colleagues and felt a daily sense of huge achievement and worth. I could not think of any other job I would rather do – I was living the dream! Why did they so confidently think that it was stress causing this dysfunction in my body? The consultant asked me to talk through what was going on in my life at that point in time, and I slowly began to list everything.

There were a number of difficult disciplinary hearings happening at the time, which was part of the fallout for why the school was in Special Measures – all of them were highly emotive and impacted across the school setting.

A significant number of teachers had handed in their notice, or were off on sick leave. No one was applying for the vacant posts because the school's reputation, as a school in crisis, was very well known throughout the area. What schools in crisis need the most is experienced teachers, but an experienced teacher knows that although they can make a huge difference, moving to a school in Special Measures (or in a challenging predicament) is not only a career gamble, it is also a wellbeing gamble.

The staff at the school felt there was no direction and had, based on previous experiences, very little trust in leadership. They were looking for a strong leader and had high demands on a number of issues within the school such as workload, communication and behaviour. Positive, embedded change in challenging circumstances takes time, but most people want it to happen overnight.

Behaviour was out of control and there had been too many exclusions to count. Not a day went by without a fight in a classroom, on the playground or in the corridors. One involved more than 20 children. Children were being sent out of classrooms to sit in the head teacher's office. No head teacher could do their job with 20 children crowded into their room. No school leader can be effective if behaviour is not controlled and managed effectively.

The surrounding community was culturally rich and diverse but also rife with many societal challenges such as finance, health and wellbeing. A road a few streets away from the school was morbidly nicknamed 'the murder mile'. When I arrived I was shown a YouTube video of a child, who had to leave the school for protection, rapping next to a burnt-out car on derelict ground, surrounded by older teens pointing a variety of firearms at the camera. Due to two areas of the city crossing over in the school's catchment area some children wore colours to school denoting which postcode they affiliated with – a very dangerous thing to do. Drugs, trafficking and violence were all regular issues discussed at the weekly police briefing held at the school. One time our local police officer bought along a colleague who told us he had 20 years' experience working as a drugs officer on Moss Side, Manchester – he grimly told us, 'This is one of the worst places I have ever worked'.

I would often walk the corridors of the school and find random people wandering around during the day looking for help or assistance. Staff were spending hours offering advice and support for housing, social care and medical issues or directing children to food banks or shelters – on a few occasions we did not have any students at the school.

The file of child protection issues at the school felt overwhelming and almost impossible to deal with appropriately. Therefore, we were making decisions where we felt outcomes were not good enough and then we saw the impact this was having on children, families and staff. It was a depressing feeling.

I knew I had the support of the Local Authority but, like so many external agencies not on the front line, they expected quick wins and improved results almost immediately. When a school is in Special Measures, even the simplest of tasks can become difficult and time consuming, and things can quickly become overwhelming because systems are either non-existent, overstretched or ineffective. It is systems, not quick fixes, that have the biggest impact in turning a struggling school into an effective one, but setting up effective systems takes time and patience.

The doctor said nothing. He did not have to.

Understand the fear – do not shut it down

I quickly realised that I was leading with fear and that this was part of the stress I was taking for granted. Fear is very real in school leadership and I needed to look at this fear and understand it. I sought professional help at this point.

1. Fear and worry are not dangerous. They are heightened feelings, and when we can gain some control over them we become more effective at leading without letting them take control of us. Things I worried about

years ago have passed and have become valuable lessons. I now see each challenge as a learning experience rather than a prison cell

2. In the moment, embrace how you are feeling. We should not fear *fear itself*. Stay with it but try to relax. I feel that staying with what worries me is one way to learn to make better decisions. I try not to think about what might happen, as this is unknown, but I do think about what I can control within the things I fear

3. I grade my anxiety in any difficult situation from one to ten (with ten being high). I find that by doing this and facing the fear, it frequently lowers over a short period. Staying in the moment and feeling the initial fear go down is a way in which I can actively gain control over how I am feeling

4. Consciously relax your muscles and learn to breathe properly. I stop and listen to my breathing and try to locate my heartbeat. Again, it is worth looking for practical advice on how to do this while you are working. Dropping my shoulders is my way of saying, ' … and relax'

Superhero syndrome

There is often a perception that it takes a superhero to come down to save the day when schools are failing or perceived to be *in trouble*. That those who turn schools around under great challenge are somehow magical or superhuman and able to do what others have failed to do. There is no doubt in my mind that leaders who are steady and turn around failing schools are people of great value to school leadership, but they are only human and this rhetoric is not helpful. What I learnt during that time in Special Measures is that it takes years and years to sustain positive change in a school, and though the leader is key, the leader's ability to lead themselves and others through that sustained change is their most important power. By trying to be a superhero I was taking power and responsibility away from others, and no single person can turn a school around.

I realised that I was stressed when working in a Special Measures environment, and who would not be? This stress was very real and it was the cause of my impotence. Therefore, my denial of the stressful situation was in fact a weakness within my leadership – not a strength as I saw it. I was blind to the stress and therefore in danger of numbing myself to the reality of the situation. I was walking into this environment every morning and learning to deaden my senses, and that was not healthy. Through soaking up the negativity, usually in the belief that I was protecting others (superhero syndrome at its worst) and somehow a stronger leader because of this, I was in fact numbing myself from the truth of the challenges we all faced and slowly adding to the problems faced by the school.

Much concerning leading a school is about feeling it and understanding the impact on the community – positive or negative. You need to be mindful that as the leader you resonate and reflect the world you are part of. When you put on your superhero cape because you are scared or you think it will help, you are teaching yourself to not feel, and in school leadership your feelings are among the most important things you have because they are a radar on your wellbeing and a spotlight on the wellbeing of your staff and community. It has taken me so long to understand that when scared as a school leader it is not about shutting that fear down, but about learning to notice it and rising up to meet it openly and transparently with the team. It is not about not being scared; it is about not letting this fear paralyse you.

A few years ago, I was talking to an ex-colleague who I taught with in London who also became a head teacher and had recently retired. I asked them how they felt now. They talked about the feeling of release that washed over them at the beginning of their retirement. When I pushed them to explain this in more detail they said that they felt like needles had been removed from their hands. That they could feel again. That each of the responsibilities that had become part of their day-to-day were slowly being removed, one by one, and they felt a huge sense of feeling coming back to them. As the responsibility had slipped away so had the need to protect themselves from fear of failure.

Experience scars

Experience scars are the remains of difficult and challenging times. I see them as a natural part of the healing process and an important segment in understanding how to lead more effectively. They can be unpleasant and leave a lasting legacy that can impact on our wellbeing and haunt us as we take on the challenges of future problems and dilemmas. I see scars as an integral part of our leader narrative, and within them there are many lessons to learn. Those narratives are an important part of who we are as 'the school leader', and time spent understanding what they mean is vital in developing how we lead. The painful scars are often the best lessons to learn from. They reflect the greatest challenges and how we managed them for better or worse. Making mistakes is something we need to come to terms with, as is doing things in a way that causes bigger problems and greater stress. Until you have had to dismiss someone, or make someone redundant, or sit across the table with a grieving parent, you do not really know how you will respond in the moment or over time. Those experience scars are a reminder and help us to find the right time to learn the lessons they hold. They do not make the experiences any easier. In fact they are a reminder of why we seek to avoid such situations. Some things in any leadership role will always be hard, but they allow us a better understanding of how we work under different pressures and what we want to change if we are in the same or similar situations in the future.

Experience scars come with a warning. Much of what we do as a leader comes from our instincts. When facing a challenging situation, we are naturally inclined to handle the circumstances in a certain way. We can feel our bodies strain when we go against our so-called better nature. We can learn from experiences, we can say that 'Next time I will do this differently', but often this goes against who we are and how we best work. Therefore, changing habits is never easy even when they are leading us to repeating mistakes. We also need to remember that scar tissue has no nerve endings. You cannot feel where you have been scarred. It should be a reminder to learn from the experience that those scars left behind rather than a badge we wear.

I am currently over eight years into my third substantive headship. I remember when I started my current post that I was very confident that I would bring all my previous experiences to bear on this new challenge. The mistakes I made in headships one and two would not be repeated in headship number three.

I could not have been more wrong.

I naturally reverted to familiar approaches of avoiding conflict, delaying difficult decisions in the hope that new solutions would appear and taking more time than colleagues wanted for me to make important decisions. These are not necessarily critical failures in leadership if managed well. I have compensated for them by ensuring that I have other senior members of staff alongside me who have different approaches, tactics and experiences but a shared vision. There is nothing wrong with trying to find ways to avoid conflict if possible – but you cannot always avoid it. Taking time to make important decisions is sometimes much better than not taking time. It is all a balancing act. The reason I am aware of these things is through reflecting on my own experiences and the scars they have left behind. Interestingly, when staff have been critical of my leadership qualities it has very rarely been these bigger aspects they have mentioned. It is more likely to be:

- You did not say 'good morning' as we passed in the corridor
- You have not replied to my email
- You were blunt in the staff meeting
- You have not acknowledged how hard I worked on this

Again, I naturally do these things – though they are much easier to work on when I become aware they are a problem. That is not to say the bigger issues do not affect staff as well – they do. But throughout my time as a school leader I have been very aware of how my actions, big or small, impact on others and what I can control in order to improve the way I lead within the context of the setting I am in. Once again, context is vitally important and there is rarely one fixed way to lead that works across schools. I do not find praising others or accepting praise easy. Therefore, I do not naturally do it often. For some staff this is a blessing because they also do not enjoy praise, especially publicly, but for others they see this as a weakness within my leadership. My brilliant governor put it this way: "I find that some people who do not enjoy praise do appreciate gratitude. These are often people with a healthy sense of self-worth. They do not seek or need praise, but they absolutely need to know you are grateful."

The wellbeing of colleagues can then become intricately woven into your wellbeing. Managing this is something that we need to learn to do – usually through the difficult lessons we learn from our leadership within the context of our school.

The naked leader

Being vulnerable as the school leader is risky and yet important. On one level, everyone wants their head teacher to be a decent human being, but on another, they want them to deal with all the difficult decisions that a school and society can throw their way. When exposed and vulnerable we can see the true mantle of the leader. The cloaks we wear are often smoke screens and our teams want to know the person beneath all this when they weather the difficult challenges. Being vulnerable is not the problem – we are all vulnerable at times, but it is how we respond during these times that are so important to others. No matter what people say, we all feel exposed and naked in tough and difficult situations. Great leaders learn to live with this vulnerability and turn it into a strength. They know how to seem to be calm, composed and clear even when every atom within them is screaming for them to panic and run for the hills.

There is a very fine line between strength and calamity though. This is why we sometimes see so much chaos and carnage scattered down the corridors of schools. Exposing leader vulnerabilities is easy enough – we can see flaws in most people's systems, strategies, communication and vision. Cracks exist everywhere and we need to learn to be comfortable with this. Rather than hide our flaws we must learn to expose them.

Getting the balance right between open and honest leadership within your role is a huge challenge. Leaders cannot spend their time complaining or being the victim. This is a very destructive trap to fall into because it leads us down a negative track. Negative leadership is a recipe for disaster. We need to think about how our own vulnerabilities can lift those around us and this means understanding what we should share with them. If we can share experiences that help others understand how we feel at the same time as communicating what we are going to do proactively to move forward, we help put challenges into perspective. There is nothing wrong with not knowing the answers imme-diately, feeling apprehensive or fearful of upcoming events. Being paralysed by them can lead to others losing confidence due to our inaction and cause additional stress to our teams. Thinking this through is important and I often talk with people outside of my school and role about how I am going to tackle challenging conversations or problems I face. It is often very surprising to hear another perspective, which suddenly makes you question your usual approach or makes perfect sense. If, in being open and honest about our vulnerability within a challenge, we can keep our dignity, respect and focus, then we move forward in a positive way. We hear it said a lot, but emotional intelligence is a vital aspect of leadership when working with as many people as we do.

O captain! My captain!

When I took on the leadership of a school in Special Measures a few days before the start of term I was asked, 'What are you going to do for the INSET?'. I had no idea and the thought filled me with panic. I tweeted for help and got a reply from the author of *Taming Tigers* and keynote speaker, Jim Lawless. I had just seen Jim deliver his keynote speech to 2,000 head teachers and could not believe it when he said he would turn up and do his keynote speech in our school for free. I remember walking on to introduce Jim to the unfamiliar small team of staff gathered in a rundown school hall and bumbled my way through some words about 'seeing the wood for the trees'. I did not know what I was trying to say and I felt a tangible fear in the pit of my stomach. Jim came on and was amazing. Every one of his rules for Taming Tigers resonated with the room: *do something scary every day, the tools for taming tigers are all around you* and *act boldly today – time is limited* screamed out to me as I watched from the wings. I caught him afterwards and he asked if he could give me some advice. Of course, I said yes. 'Brian, when the ship is sinking no one wants to look to the captain and see fear in their eyes or hear it in their voice.'

The honesty of it hurt, but it was a vital piece of information which I have taken with me far into my time as a school leader. In the following weeks, I took on the task with renewed insight, knowing that leading through the coming storm would need everyone on hand to be feeling fit, healthy and ready for the challenge ahead. I knew that how they saw me mattered and I needed to instil a sense of calm and confidence in challenging times. How I presented myself to others would be incredibly important in achieving this. The head teacher role can be likened to that of a captain of a ship. You can steer anywhere you want, but you need a deep understanding of navigation skills if you want to get to your destination. Most people can point in the direction they want to go and aim for it. Steering without knowledge and understanding is a dangerous thing to do. You need to be able to decode the sun–shadow board as the clouds gather, or translate the colour of the sea and the wind's direction.

You need to understand when the crew are tired, scared or bored. The wisdom of your experience scars is a crucial tool in plotting that destination as well. What Jim's words taught me was that I needed the expertise of others to be a better captain, rather than feel that my every word was what they wanted to hear. I needed to use my leadership skills to build a team that could also navigate and pilot the ship without me and trust the decisions of their leadership in helping them to do this, even when they felt that fear well up in the pit of their stomach.

Some mistakes are bigger than others, and through taking a careful and reflective approach to the way we lead in times of success and failure we need to learn not to place too much of our energy into punishing ourselves or going through some sort of narcissistic drama. Often when the mistakes become apparent there is little we can do and we have to move on quickly. We also have to take others along that same journey; we have to find ways in which they commit to and believe in the vision we have. Being sucked up into the tornado of a mistake can be extremely damaging, especially if it becomes caught up in a personal narrative rather than a collective one. I have seen many people try to hold together a flimsy excuse only to end up making a much bigger mess than if they had accepted and apologised for the first mistake.

I have felt fear in my role many times when the realisation has hit that because of previous mistakes made I was now facing an avalanche of problems. It starts in the pit of the stomach and rises up into the chest. These are always critical times because I have since learnt that what I do next is very important. Acting in this state of fear can create all sorts of additional problems that start a cycle of new challenges that help give the fear an upper hand. In some circumstances the original fear could be a tiny one but could end up creating a host of new fears that could build up and overwhelm if we are not careful. I have seen this happen in moments where a situation with parents escalated into conflict and I have seen it happen slowly over the course of a year. We have to control our fears if we are going to be able to tackle the long list of challenges we face as school leaders. Living in fear is one of the most limiting conditions you can have in trying to improve a school.

I have always been honest about the mistakes I make, the flaws I see in my leadership and the areas that I need to work on. This leaves me vulnerable at times but ultimately I see it as a strength for moving forward and I associate it with my longevity in the role. By naming our fears, in the right circles of support, we enable ourselves to face up to them. It allows others in, such as your leadership team or chair of governors, and, as long as it's not self-pitying, experience tells me they will be quick to help you find positive solutions. It is only when your mistakes become a melodrama centred around your inflated sense of importance that the empathy of others fades. That's when talk of a mutiny begins.

Culture club

The wellbeing of the people in your team is one of the most important invest-ments you can make as a leader; it is also one of the most complex to manage. Everyone is different and what works for one person may not work for another. On a personal level, I would feel physically sick if I was expected to attend a work-related relaxation class or yoga session with colleagues. I could not think of anything that would put me into more of a sweat and make me feel as ter-rified. Therefore, I believe that you need to get wellbeing right in the everyday culture and ethos of your school.

Too often I have heard words to the effect of 'We are doing this for the chil-dren!' from school leaders – sometimes, as the bloody knife is thrust into the back of some poor, unsuspecting member of staff. Now, you could ask, 'What is wrong with this?'. 'For the children!' is a perfectly good ethos to have as some-one who leads a school. In fact, it's part of our core duty. I see it differently: I have always felt that the role of the head teacher is to 'Do it for the staff' – for good reason. If we look after our staff, then you can pretty much guarantee that they can be focused on their job, which is about providing a quality education for children.

Embedding an ethos that puts wellbeing into the day-to-day culture of the school's daily routines and practices is an important way to achieve this. Building a whole-school culture where everyone is responsible for each other's wellbeing is more effective than bringing in initiatives and schemes that are usually time limited, unsustainable or niche. They can be unsettling, whereas an ethos that looks at teachers' use of time, basic behaviours and realistic expectations from senior leaders, if consistent, can make a world of difference to how everyone feels. An effective leader needs to promote wellbeing and champion it through practices that they can model.

A great example of this is time spent on administration tasks such as mark-ing and assessment. Both are important aspects of being a good teacher but too often are done without thinking about their purpose from the perspective of the teacher. When we strip away aspects of the role that do not really impact on teaching and learning in productive ways then we begin to build a team with purpose.

Conclusion: Top five tips for thinking about your wellbeing

Much can be said about wellbeing and, as I stated at the beginning of this chapter, I believe that it is an area very poorly dealt with because it is often about individual need. You can highlight its impact and raise awareness about it, but to effectively deal with it in a high-pressure school environment needs nuance and a good understanding of your individual staff needs. Following are five key areas to explore when thinking about wellbeing.

5. Find your tribe

Other school leaders might not know your context but they will know what it feels like to face a difficult challenge within a school environment. They will know what you mean when you say that you think you are a fraud. Leaders are constantly discovering the many ambiguities and joys of leadership, as you are, even when your outcomes and experiences differ. Finding other leaders to become part of your conversations is incredibly important in the good times but especially so during the more difficult times. Knowing that you are not alone is paramount throughout your career – not just in the early days of school leadership. Other leaders have rescued me on countless occasions in the past, from sage words of advice to sharing a letter they wrote or through emailing over their head teacher reports or School Development Plans. One of the best learning experiences is visiting another school (preferably one very different from mine) and looking at how they organise their communication board in the staffroom. I have learnt so many new ways of sharpening communication across the school site – just by looking at how the week was presented to staff. I cannot reiterate this strongly enough; school leadership can be the loneliest job so it is vital we find people who know what it is like to face Ofsted, ranting parents or a bereaved child so we can do the toughest things knowing that others have been there. Just speaking to someone on the phone who has got through a similar challenge to the one you are facing is extremely valuable.

A good place to start is your local schools. I found that in previous headships my local heads became incredibly important in helping to get to know the area and understand so many of the issues within the town, city or local authority. You can also look to that group of leaders you developed with – for example if you were a deputy, you will find that colleagues here also become school leaders (and they are often still vitally important when they do not). I have found my support network on courses, at the gym (a bit weird) and through mutual friends.

4. Strategic sanctuary

One of the early traps in leadership is trying to please everyone all of the time. It is a conundrum that will follow you until your retirement – even when you know you cannot it is always there in the back of your mind. Often, while trying to fit all the pieces together to best please everyone we water down the impact we would have had if we had gone with our original plan. That is not to say exploring different options is not a good idea – it is. However, as a school leader we need to face up to difficult decisions early on and learn to deal with them on a personal and executive level. This is often where having a mentor or coach helps. People with whom we talk through the decisions we are going to make and the impact this will have. I have heard it called 'strategic sanctuary'. A sandbox place where we are free to voice our thoughts and ideas without fear of others ridiculing them or being upset by them. Another of the big well-being pressures on a school is during any change of management procedure. Having a safe place to take our plans and discuss them is extremely important and sometimes this needs to be away from our own school. It does not take away the difficult decisions, but it allows us time to gain an understanding and therefore be better briefed about what we are taking on.

A good question to ask is:

What can we control here, and what is out of our control?

3. A work in progress

The idea that when you become head teacher you are the finished article is a very dangerous one, and yet many people will treat you as though you have all the answers and information for every problem that presents itself. Letting others know that you do not have the answer right now or it is unlikely you will ever have the answer is not a weakness. Looking to others for the answer is also a sign of strength and better for the school than trying to prove a point. Again, we need to be honest and look at how we can use our strengths within a situation to support, even if we do not have the direct answer that someone is looking for. This can be as simple as, 'No, I don't know where the cleaning products are kept but if you ask in the office I am sure they will', or 'I have no idea how to implement Rosenshine's Principles of Instruction into a geography lesson, but I am sure that there is someone out there who does'. We need to allow our staff to see us as human rather than pretend we are the font of all knowledge.

2. Teachers teach - leaders lead

This point is a controversial one because I have heard many head teachers and teachers say how important it is that a head teacher can show that they can still teach. I believe that when you become the school leader you need to hone your leadership knowledge and skills, not your class-based teaching knowledge and skills. Part of that is understanding how teaching and learning works within the context of your school but you are *not* a teacher. Even if you have a small teaching commitment, your role is different. Teachers live and breathe the art and craft of teaching and learning each and every day; they plan it, deliver it and mark it. Leaders might go into the classroom and take a class, but it is not what your job description asks and ultimately it is not what your community expects you to do. I have not taught a class for years (I do not count a cover lesson as being a teacher) but I have spent years leading teaching and learning. I need to use my leadership skills to empower teachers to do what they do best through sharpening the craft of leading an effective school. That is why I find that one of the biggest issues that impact on teachers' wellbeing – lesson observations and the monitoring of learning in their classroom and therefore performance management – needs to be about understanding teachers' skills and knowledge supported by your experience and wisdom in the context of your school. Leaders need to acknowledge that this should be a robust conversation in which they are well informed but trying to understand the practical challenges the teacher is facing and how best to support them through this for better outcomes.

Although school leaders are rarely teachers any more (sorry small school head teachers – that's a whole chapter right there) it is important that we justify and question every new initiative with an understanding of what it is to be a teacher in our school. Through doing this we can have an immense impact on the wellbeing of our teachers. I have learnt that the happier my teachers are with their workload and role, the happier I am with mine.

1. It is just a job

My father told me how, at the end of his shift working as a supervisor in a factory, whether nights or days, he would walk to his car and refuse to put the key into the ignition until he was happy that he was going to leave work behind. Sometimes he would sit there for over 30 minutes. In teaching, from the earliest stages there is a pervasive culture that the job always lives with us. Taking work home, marking and planning over weekends and coming in during the holidays are spoken about as if they are the norm within teaching. Some even go as far as wearing them as badges of honour. I believe that this narrative can be a very destructive one. I go out of my way to make sure work does not follow me home like some sort of wellbeing assassin, and in doing this I do my best to ensure my staff also feel that they have control over their workload.

I have found that when my working life takes control of my family life, we all suffer. The arguments of 'you don't understand' or 'I have to' creep in and chip away at two of the most important foundations to ensuring you do a good job: that you feel well and in control within your role and your personal life; that you feel happy. If I am not well then how can I lead others to be well? Therefore, I have to put the job into perspective. I have to organise my working week so that I do the things that need to be done as a priority. I would rather work late than take work home. Making my home a place where I can take off the cloak of 'being head teacher' has become one of the driving factors in my longevity. It has not always been easy. It is harder when you start a new job, or you are under challenging circumstances and feel the number of tasks to do is limitless. It gets easier the longer you are in the post but you have to work hard at it. I remember once taking a call from Ofsted when I was on holiday in France. I can still picture my wife's unforgiving stare. Now, I would make sure that this conversation happened when I was back in 'role'. There was nothing I could have done about the issue while in France, apart from worry about what I was unable to do. I feel that this approach to our work as school leaders is driven by an, at times, almost insane moral drive that makes school leaders act in irrational ways. We put so much emphasis upon our conscience to do the 'right thing' that it ends up controlling our actions. The problem is your actions will never appease your conscience and therefore you create an endless loop draining your time and resolve. Ask teachers and school leaders how many hours they work and you usually get silly numbers, sometimes said with pride. But why? How many of those hours were vital or important and how many were habits in which if it did not happen no one would really notice or care? What difference do these extra hours give to the children we work with? Alternatively, if I carry on working like this will I be well enough to keep doing the basics? Having an honest and brutally analytical look at the hours we spend on our job can be very interesting. What did you do today that when under the microscope was in fact not necessary? What did you do today that was vital? Understanding and managing this can have a profound impact on our wellbeing, inside and outside of school.

Our wellbeing is absolutely vital if we want to lead successfully and over time. It's not scented baths or long walks that will keep us leading our schools (though they may help). To lead well we must learn to understand our fears and weaknesses and be able to hold them up in front of us and face them.

4
On Inclusion

This chapter will cover the importance of inclusive, diverse and equitable practice in our schools and the many challenges this can bring to our leadership. It will cover:

- The importance of understanding what inclusive practice looks like in the context of our school
- The role of the school leader in setting the standards of inclusion while also being aware of the impact this has on staff and the wider school community
- How to open up, learn from and be transparent about our inclusive, diverse or equitable (or not so) practice

The inclusion paradox

This chapter is about inclusion, a vital component in running a good and effective school. Creating a sense of belonging within and beyond the boundaries of our school is a fundamental cog in the system of good educational leadership. Inclusion should be the cornerstone on which we build upon our values, knowing that what we do within our school should be more than a positive reflection of society; that it should be a guiding light within it.

The problem with inclusion is that there is so much confusion around the issue in schools. This is especially true regarding expectations around behaviour and special educational needs. I have never heard anyone argue against trying to be inclusive, but when inclusion creates complex problems you can see arguments for it unravel and fall apart. I have seen and heard school leaders use inclusion as the reason to create systems that exclude the most vulnerable pupils, deliberately and inadvertently. Systems that create inflexible rules that do not flinch or stray which on the surface seem fair but by their very nature are not inclusive. This inclusion paradox is at the heart of many school leader debates. How do we get it right? Is it zero tolerance or unconditional regard? Does a haircut matter? Do we challenge homophobic language in school and beyond the school gates? Life is full of rules – so why should school be any different?

The ideas that form our approaches to inclusion in our school need to be nuanced and wide ranging. Inclusion is not just about money and status, though we know that a lack of inclusion is a breeding ground for poverty and prejudice; it is not limited to behaviour or special educational needs and disabilities (SEND) within a school. Inclusion is also about diversity and equity and how we lead in these areas. It is about how we create or adjust our rules, systems and values to ensure that everyone has fair access to an education, which gives them the best chances they can have. There are few things worthier to get right in our school leadership, or as challenging and complicated.

Inclusion is different from diversity, which is also often caught up in any explanations about what inclusion means. As American activist Vernā Myers told the Cleveland Bar Association in 2016, 'diversity is being invited to the party; inclusion is being asked to dance' (Cho, 2016). This is why I put inclusion first, because it is usually about lived experiences. This is why I always consider whether our community is experiencing inclusion in their everyday lived experiences, through our approaches to diversity and equity.

So you think you are inclusive?

I was showing a secondary head teacher around my school when the light-bulb moment happened. We were in one of the wide corridors of my school, especially built so that children with disabilities could get around safely, and a child from our specialist provision was being supported as she walked along the corridor. The physio had unstrapped her from the metal frame that she was usually secured into and was carefully holding her up with the assistance of a hoist. Ever so carefully the physio was walking backwards with the child's feet on top of hers, one step at a time. Coming down the corridor was a tall and immaculately dressed Year 6 girl with a violin case slung over her shoulder. She stopped, crouched down so that she was at eye level with her peer and said with a huge warm smile, 'Good morning!'. They then both had a quick hug and slowly went on their way. The secondary head turned to me and smiled. I think he thought I had set up this scenario to show off how inclusive my school was. What my colleague did not know was that both of these children needed that friendship and interaction. Both of them had recently overcome massive struggles in their lives. One had a complex medical need that meant she would never walk unaided and lived with fluctuating pain, the other had recently lost her mother and was trying to live with the grief. One inclusion issue was there for everyone to see, but the other was buried deep down in the emotions of a child trying to act 'normal'.

I realised in that moment that inclusion was not just about trying to make other people's lives better, but about the interactions we all have and need to make our own lives feel better as well. I believe that there is a perception that inclusion is only about helping others in need; this is a dangerous mindset because it ignores the fact that through striving to be inclusive everyone gains from it if we get it right. That deep down most of us thrive on the connections we have in our daily lives and we all have a desire to help others. This desire to connect and help is at the heart of being inclusive and it should not be a one-way street.

Inclusion is tough to get right. It is very rarely as simple and wonderful as that passing moment.

In my experience, inclusion comes with all sorts of problems and compli-cations, and getting it right is hard because the systems we set up, in fact the society we live in, can never be equitable. To be fair to all, they need to be flexible in different circumstances and therefore no one system works without interpretation. We do not live in an equal society, and while schools try to be inclusive places you will always be fighting against a tide of inequality, exclu-sion, poverty, apathy and anger. Despite all of this, crafting an inclusive culture is one of the most important things you will ever do as a school leader. If your inclusion does not make a difference, if it does not make life better for people, then it has little value.

What is inclusion?

The National Headteacher Standards 2020 do not directly define inclusion. They briefly mention it within the section on 'Culture and Ethos', saying that head teachers:

> Promote positive and respectful relationships across the school community and a safe, orderly and inclusive environment. (Department for Education (DfE), 2020a)

There is a lot to this statement. It implies that inclusion should be weaved into the fabric of your educational leadership. Much of this is about our basic rights to positive, safe and respectful relationships. Inclusion is the very soul of the culture and ethos you will create within your school. Without it you cannot have a vision for your school that will empower and deliver a just, safe and effective education. The SEND Code of Practice states that 'every teacher is a teacher of SEND' (Department for Education (DfE), 2020b). In the same vein, I believe that every school leader *must* be a leader of inclusion.

As human beings we need to believe that the boundaries that hold us back can be overcome, that the limits we face today will be the memories and lessons of tomorrow. Inclusion questions what we can and cannot do, no matter our circumstances. When the school leader begins to have a vision for inclusion they start to ask questions about the lived experiences within their community, and this opens up universal themes about prejudice, expectations and aspirations. What a vision for inclusion does is embed universal expectations that the knowledge and skills that enable a better life can be gained by everyone. It does not make excuses and is not afraid to stand up to age-old systems that create bias or inequality. It means we begin to think about an end point, and that must always be: How can our inclusive culture and ethos bring about a better future for everyone attending our school? You could go further and say, 'bring about a better future for society'. We might not be able to immediately change the world but we can take steps to develop people who will. For many children, especially those who live within more deprived communities, face physical or mental health challenges or daily prejudice, getting this right so that they can thrive is absolutely the gold standard in school leadership. While educational establishments like Harvard believe they are creating world leaders, most schools should have an ambition of creating better citizens who have the power to effectively challenge prejudice and inequality and champion diversity because they will change the world.

It's a hard knock life

My first teaching job was on an estate in south Bristol where more than 70% of the children received free school meals. This area highlighted the absolute inequalities of wealth within the small city of Bristol, where a short bus ride would take you to some of the wealthiest areas of the country. A head teacher is almost always schooled as a classroom teacher. It is the place where many of our core beliefs as educators form and are nurtured into our leadership beliefs. Working on this estate I learnt much about how poverty drains ambition through the generations; how financial hardship breeds other problems such as domestic violence, substance abuse and crime as well as one of the most destructive – a lack of educational ambition. This is an important point. In all areas where I have worked there has been ambition, but the idea that education is an ambition worthy of attention has sometimes been hard to find in the most deprived areas I have worked in.

Education rarely delivers the quick win – one of the first things a teacher truly gets to understand about learning is it takes time, perseverance and hard work. I remember one of my pupils telling me about how his brother was able to get cheap PlayStation games while on the dole and play them all day: 'He's living the dream, Sir!' I am very careful not to stereotype here, but having worked in many communities where poverty was a stark reality the idea of doing what you want to do (no matter how naive this may be) was a powerful dream.

I always struggled to sell the dreams of academic success against the National Lottery, or perceived quick achievements like Love Island, You Tubing, TikTok or other seemingly easy wins: the overnight success stories that are streamed through the consciousness of many young minds. Of course, apart from the lottery, which still needs some form of dedication, what was often missed was how there is rarely ever an overnight success without a backbone of hard work – that, like with any ambition, we almost always have to work hard to achieve the goals we want. Again, where we can struggle in education is selling a degree in mathematics over the multi-million-pound dream of being a coder on the next *Grand Theft Auto*. It's the role of the teacher to get across just how hard that dream for success will be to achieve; it has always been the same for those who dream of being a professional footballer (millions of children) – there is no easy way to achieve this, and if you don't have the ability to work hard and the resilience to see your dreams through, you have little chance of success. What we have to learn when ensuring that inclusion is at the heart of our educational vision is how to get pupils to understand that the leg work they put in at school is seen as the building blocks to later success in life. That can be a very hard dream to sell. Therefore, you need to make sure that ambition and hard work run through the very fabric of your school. It has to be more than a slogan, or a policy. It has to be chiselled into the DNA, words and actions of everyone who works in the school. They need to believe it.

I remember sitting at the bus stop opposite my first school as a teacher; the pub behind me had a Union Jack flag that had seen better days, hanging limp and lifeless. There were rumours about the pub's right-wing connections – it was where many of our parents drank. There were burnt-out stolen cars, the aftermath of joy rides, that would lie on the nearby abandoned ground for months before the council would remove them. I would often walk past the smouldering remains in the morning as I walked into the school's car park and then sometimes I would see children from my school on top of the burnt-out remains having the time of their lives when they should have been having breakfast and getting ready for school.

Much of this life would spill over into the playground, sometimes between children, sometimes between the parents themselves. There was a sense of a 'this is how it is' acceptance. No one talked about how education was the ticket out. Back then the only ticket people mentioned was the National Lottery. Rarely did I have conversations with parents that focused on education as a future answer. As a destination, we mostly talked about the past or the current problems facing the family. I quickly learnt as a teacher that one of the most powerful tools I had was finding the positives within children's academic work and behaviour – highlighting progress and bringing conversations with parents around to learning and attitudes rather than other distractions or excuses. This was because in many cases education was not seen as a viable option because the parents' experiences of education were not positive ones. They had no experiences that led them to place their faith in the idea that working hard in school would create pathways out of poverty and inequality.

I know this from personal experience. My mother left school at 15 to have me. She worked hard as I grew up, holding down many cleaning jobs, and my father worked long shifts at the local Milk Marketing Board. I knew, growing up, that I was expected to leave school as soon as I could and get a job. I saw, or was told about, no other avenue. There was an industrial estate nearby and I always knew that this was where I would end up, even when I was in primary school. My mother phoned up to get me an interview there not long after leaving secondary school. I do not think my parents ever went to a parents' evening when I was at secondary school. They never spoke about formal education in a positive way. They did not have positive memories of school. They wanted me to earn money; they saw this as a better life, as 'getting on'. They wanted me to be able to buy a house on the estate, settle down, have children and be happy. There is nothing wrong with this dream. However, when poverty and inequality surround you it can be hard to see education as the answer without someone you trust shining a light upon it and championing it with lived experiences. In fact, today for many parents the idea that their child will do well at GCSEs and A-levels and then go on to university is about accepting that there will be debt, a lot of it – and for many families who have experienced poverty, why aspire to this? because to fail is almost unthinkable. It is very hard to sell the academic dream on the back of this, and many systems set up in society only make this more apparent:

I always just thought the aim was to dismantle poverty. However, once you see the mechanics of the poverty industry up close, you realise it's in the state of permanent growth and that without individuals, families and communities in crisis there would no longer be a role for these massive institutions. (McGarvey, 2017)

Behaviour and exclusions

Another massive issue around inclusive practice is that it is often confused with placement. It can be dominated by the very tricky issue of inclusion's nemesis, exclusion. This can water down the key principles you need to embed while trying to achieve inclusive practice across an organisation. An exclusion (now officially called suspension), especially a permanent exclusion of a child from your school, is deeply emotive, and should be one of the toughest decisions you make as a school leader. At its heart it is something you have to be clear and consistent about, and yet every time it presents itself to you it creates dilemmas and nuances that rip through the school and wider community in moments. Not getting on top of behaviour can be a disaster for the school leader. Over the years I have seen many school leaders leave the profession over exclusion problems because they could not get behaviour right. As hard as it is, no school leader should ever be afraid to say that a particular placement at their school is not working, but I also believe they have to prove that they tried to make it work. I have sat on countless SEND panel meetings where it was clear the school did everything to try to make a placement work but it still failed. I have also sat at meetings where exclusion was the first, last and only approach for any behaviour that strayed from the school rules. This inconsistency is local and nationwide. What one school does can be a million miles from what another would do. Even the debate about behaviour is so polarised that it is almost impossible to reach a consensus on what should happen around behaviour rules in our schools.

I believe that inclusion is not a free-for-all mishmash of acceptance. As school leaders we have to be very clear on what is acceptable and not acceptable in our schools. We owe this to the children, staff and community. It comes down to the rules that we put in place and making sure everyone understands them and rigorously adheres to them once they are set – otherwise what is the point of setting them in the first place? I have three school rules and they are easy for anyone to remember:

- Be kind
- Be safe
- Be responsible

I know this is not an exhaustive list. I know that they do not cover every aspect of what it is to be a successful citizen. I can use these rules though in almost all circumstances, and therefore I have a consistent language across the school. It gives me a way to communicate to all children, even nursery children and those with complex special educational needs. It is vitally important that we start with rules that are easy to understand and promote. They need to be so clear that everyone can understand them and therefore use them on a daily basis.

When there is a behaviour issue in my school now I will always start with which rule has been broken:

- You weren't safe because you ran out of the classroom and hid
- You were unkind because of the words you used
- You weren't responsible and you haven't finished your work in class this morning

This language can change to meet age, ability or even communication needs. We use the same rules in our mainstream school as we do in nursery and specialist provision. Being able to find examples for these three simple rules has never been a problem. I always use assemblies to illustrate the rules and constantly ask children what they are and to give me an example of what it is to be kind, safe or responsible in school and beyond. Clarity is at the heart of inclusion, and when I see it go wrong it is often because that coherence has been lost and there is confusion about systems and procedures. Inclusion is about being connected to your place and feeling valued there as well as being able to see the links beyond it that make what you do and learn relevant. You can create a safe place through clarity of rules and expectations, and when everyone knows and understands the rules you are much further along the road to having a calmer and more inclusive school.

This might seem like a very obvious and simple take on inclusion, but when I go in to support schools where behaviour is a barrier I always ask the leaders, children and staff what the school rules are. I often see long lists with a host of very specific rules. I also see that each group has a different list, and children see it differently than senior leaders, or teachers. Some lists I have seen would take a grandmaster at chess to memorise. As soon as rules become something that are not simple to remember and understand they can become ineffective. If everyone in the school cannot recite the school rules, I can almost guarantee that you will find a lack of transparency over expectations of behaviour, and as soon as this happens the system begins to unravel. This will lead to variance within the language used to deal with behaviour and ultimately it will mean that there is a lack of unity around supporting children and staff. In schools where there is unity on the rules, where they are clear and well-presented, there is almost always a sense of calm, even in schools where behaviour is a challenge.

I have been in some of the most challenging Pupil Referral Units (PRU) and they are often havens of calm, despite the fact that very challenging behaviour can be triggered within seconds and many of the young people in them have a history of struggling against school rules. The best ones are where children know how the staff will respond and the staff all know that each and every one of them know how they will respond. PRUs are sometimes seen as the afterthoughts of inclusion, a place for children when everything has broken down, and yet I believe that many hold the key to best inclusive practice.

I am not saying that to get inclusion right, to ensure that there are no exclusions in schools, we all have to run our schools in the same way a PRU would. That's not feasible, and PRUs have freedoms and tolerances that would be extremely hard to replicate within mainstream settings. Neither am I saying that if you exclude a child you have failed on inclusion. The brutal fact is that there are times when an exclusion is the only answer a school has to problems that can damage the very soul of a school. This is the reason why every school leader has to get behaviour right in their school. If an exclusion happens it must be a last resort which should hurt to do and seem like an impossible decision. Exclusion is a necessary procedure though, one that school leaders need to take in cases where the system, despite their best efforts, is unable to meet the needs of a child who puts themselves and others at constant risk. I believe that this has never been more important than it is now. If a suspension or permanent exclusion is a graduated response where it is clear that the school has acted in good faith to get things right, no school leader should feel bad, or be questioned on this important aspect of what they need to do in the best interests of the school community. Sadly, too many outside of running schools fail to understand this – therefore, school leaders are always under huge pressure when this decision has to be taken.

Another important issue around dealing with complex behaviours and children at risk of exclusion is capacity. It is about understanding your capacity to meet the challenges you have. We need to think about the systems we have in finer detail. How are we set up so that we can be inclusive and create a school ethos in which everyone has the chance to feel accepted and provided for within a place and a time? This cannot be fixed, but can be a system with some flexibility and fluidity allowing for reasonable adjustments without taking away the basic rules. I have always covered this by making sure capacity is always on the agenda when meeting with my senior leaders. You can think about capacity in a structural way, but when you see it from an operational perspective you realise it is never set and static and therefore it needs constant attention.

Quality teaching is the most powerful tool we have to enable an inclusive environment

With all this in mind I take a strategic look at behaviour within my school. It is something I think very carefully about and often review – creating a positive and supportive environment which understands what the barriers to learning are.

When we get positive relationships right that is because there is a good understanding of expectations, the rules and where support can be found when it is needed. The teacher's greatest weapon in education is having the knowledge, skill, time and understanding to teach great lessons without distractions. Positive relationships are not about teachers having to constantly adjust to more and more challenging behaviours or deliver lessons without support. Teaching has always been about teacher knowledge, relationships and active engagement; get this right and your school will flourish very quickly. Through inclusion, build capacity for individuals to be independent of support and know what success looks like for them – to make them want to go beyond what they thought was possible. Quite simply, make them want to be in class learning and understand why this really matters to them.

Knowing the needs of the pupils in your school and building your provision so that it can directly address those needs is a vital strategic priority. But you also need to set high expectations so that they know that you expect them to go beyond what they are doing. It is sometimes easy for the school leader to base their provision upon loose principles, or best-practice statements. These are usually sweeping statements about being 'world class' and they are meaningless to the vast majority of your school community. Get provision right, get teaching right and ensure that teachers have the time, space and knowledge to know the individuals in their classroom; setting high expectations and providing the right teaching is critical in being inclusive. It should be at the front of every leader's strategy. It is about how you support but also how you monitor and set the expectations for teaching and learning in your school. This will be contextual, different for each and every school. Therefore, inclusion that makes a difference is about teaching and learning.

Teachers play a key role in supporting behaviour, but to create positive and supportive environments school leaders must ensure that they are given the time and space to teach so they can build positive cultures within their classroom. Ensuring that pupils have access to high-quality teaching is probably the first long-term priority a school leader should have. Get this right and many of the challenges will melt away. The danger here is balancing supporting your teachers with behaviour so they can teach, alongside empowering your teachers to deal with behaviour. At all my schools, it has been vital that senior leaders are visible and available when teachers need them. I cannot think of anything worse for a teacher than being alone to deal with escalating disruptive behaviour while trying to teach. However, senior leaders being called to a classroom because a child flicked a pen top waters down teacher authority and hands over problems. We work hard to give teachers autonomy and follow up with parents and, over time, we know in almost all cases that when senior leaders are called, it is because the issue needs them to deal with it.

Celebrating diversity: How to talk about race and ethnicity in school

In education 'inclusion' is often described as the right of parents and children to access mainstream education alongside their peers. Inclusion is far more universal than this though. It is not just about learning and behaviour needs. It is about celebrating diversity which, in turn, grows safe, positive and nurturing environments. It means understanding one another by exceeding simple definitions of tolerance to ensure that people truly value their and others' differences. This allows us both to clasp onto and celebrate the rich dimensions of variety contained within each and every individual and expect that the ethos of our school is one of acceptance, growth, knowledge and progression.

Therefore, we need to learn from our most uncomfortable lessons.

I sat at my school desk reading an email from a former student of the school, Shalana Serafina Bharath:

> *I am writing to you today, following the recent death of George Floyd, an African American man who was murdered at the hands of a white police officer in Minnesota on the 25th of May 2020. For the first time in my existence, I have found a confidence within me to address the distressing issues that I have felt, and am still feeling as a person of colour, due to the triggering exposure that George Floyd's death has created within the media.*

I paused, wondering where this letter would take me, immediately feeling out of my depth. Although I have worked in diverse communities such as Brick Lane in Tower Hamlets and Easton in Central Bristol and I have been a trustee for charities such as Think Global and Young Citizens, which schooled me through first-hand experiences of fighting for justice and advocacy, I realise I am not comfortable discussing race with people of colour. It is not something I do, ever. What I did not realise, as I began reading these emails, is what a profound impact having this conversation would have on me.

> *When it came to my race, I was unsure as to who I could turn to when I was upset at school. All my friends were white, all my teachers were white, all my dinner ladies were white, so as a child, I felt my racial*

experiences couldn't be discussed on a one to one basis. I accept now, that this was because I didn't want to make anyone feel uncomfortable. Unfortunately, this feeling of not wanting to make anyone feel uncomfortable or embarrassed followed me through into my adult life. I think it's rather worrying that at the age of 27, I now feel ready to talk, but I want to use my voice today, because I do not want fellow school students to feel the same way that I did at primary school.

I began to compose my reply and immediately felt that my words had little meaning or impact:

As a white working class boy growing up on a Somerset estate I had always thought I understood how hard it was to succeed in life. I have been shocked to my core by what happened to George Floyd, not because it surprised me … but to think I was also shocked by Rodney King's beating at the hands of the LAPD when I was a young teenager and yet … here we are, nothing has changed. It is only recently in these last few weeks that I can now see the difference that white privilege has brought me. I was poor, my mother had me at 16, both my parents left school with no qualifications … but still I had white privileges. I did not grow up in a system that was set up to make my life even harder than it should be.

What was I trying to say in this reply? Was I trying to justify my place in all this by making out, 'Hey, it was tough for me too'? What has that got to do with anything? Having read 'Why I am no longer talking to white people about race' by Reni Eddo-Lodge, wasn't that their point about most white people?

They've never had to think about what it means, in power terms, to be white, so any time they're vaguely reminded of this fact, they interpret it as an affront. Their eyes glaze over in boredom or widen in indignation. Their mouths start twitching as they get defensive. Their throats open up as they try to interrupt, itching to talk over you but not to really listen, because they need to let you know you have got it wrong. (Eddo-Lodge, 2014)

As I tried to deflect how uncomfortable I felt I replied with a question:

What would help me would be to think what would have made a difference for you when you were here?

The ex-student's reply in her next email, so simple and yet so profound, left me feeling overwhelmed because it was so obvious. You see, I should have never needed to ask that question. Why does something so fundamentally easy to understand have to be explained?

White teachers not being afraid to have a sit down, one to one discussion with a child from a minority background.

Not being afraid. There it is again. Fear, a warning and a prison. I realised just how afraid I was of getting it wrong, upsetting others, seeming to be uncultured, ignorant, stupid or – even worse – at heart a racist. I remember the earliest days of my headship in Tower Hamlets – on the last day of term, everyone jubilant, handing out presents and saying goodbyes for the summer holidays. The teaching assistants were all hugging and, feeling the love in the room, I approached my female Muslim TA who had been the most amazing person to work with. I felt such admiration for her. I stepped forward to hug her, arms out wide and she stepped back, shock in her eyes; then the terrible and awkward silence. I had learnt nothing. I should have known that what I proposed was wrong on many levels, but still I stumbled into this mistake as though I could change the rules. It was my mistake but everyone was embarrassed. How could I have been so foolish? What was worse is she tried to make me feel better by explaining things. I said it was OK and we moved on. If only I had the confidence to sit down and understand why I had got it wrong and show that I had learnt from it in the moment.

The correspondence between us continued to open my eyes and make me reflect on some uncomfortable truths.

At school, children were always told off or punished for throwing me casually racist comments, but I was never then approached by a senior member of staff to see if I was OK. Most of the time they probably thought I was, because I'd been conditioned to brush comments like that under the carpet, but deep down I would have loved for someone to reach out and just check in on me. I don't know if it was assumed, but I don't think teachers should assume that we would have gone home to our parents to discuss racism, or nasty comments at school.

The power that teachers and school staff have is so evident in these words. It was also clear that ignoring the issues through a fear that we could potentially get it wrong, or failing to open up a conversation we felt uneducated to deal with, was a bigger crime. A crime of ignorance which excluded a child. As a teacher, the fear of being accused of racism or being culturally ignorant is a terrifying one. I have very rarely met a teacher who does not want to do the best they can, but how much do many of us know about black or minority history, how well read are we? What do we know about the fundamental issues impacting upon the contextual realities for families in the areas we teach in – including the wider national ones? I was very well read in poverty or working-class culture, but this is clearly not the same. As teachers and school leaders we should be educated in our real history and see black and minority history as British history, and then we can be a little more confident speaking to others about race.

We're always told from a young age that 'sticks and stones may break my bones, but words will never hurt me', but words do hurt, as much as you pretend that they don't. In reference to my last email, as a young child I probably felt that I couldn't have approached a white senior member of staff about my upset with racist comments because I would have been worried that I would have made my white teachers feel uncomfortable.

By this point I was emotionally burnt out. I don't want to play into the white guilt narrative, but the next part, as someone who has dedicated their career to education, knocked me for six:

At school, when I was in Year 6, we did an end of school show. The show was Snow White and our teachers held auditions for each of us. Being a budding performer I would have killed to have the lead role, but I distinctly remember not auditioning for Snow White because I knew there would be no chance of me getting the role of a character that had 'skin as white as snow'. I remember casually saying this to a friend in front of a teacher. Looking back now, I wish that the teacher would have been brave enough to sit me down and discuss the comment that I had just made, even though it was a flippant remark. To perhaps tell me that I could have still auditioned for that role despite my race would have taught me to think outside the box and not limit myself because of my skin colour.

As school leaders we must be open about how we create an ethos within our schools that gets the best from all children. We may think we are doing what is best for a child by either believing we are protecting them from harm, avoiding the embarrassment of an unfamiliar discussion or thinking we are not skilled enough to have these conversations; however, leaders, by our very nature, must want the children we educate to be the better versions of ourselves. Not some children – *all* children. We must think beyond our own limitations to make this happen. We must think big at all times – that has got to be our goal – more so now than ever before. By avoiding talking about experiences outside of our comfort zones or not really listening to the experiences of others, we go nowhere, backwards. We just continue to accept the status quo rather than be the key lever for change in a child's life.

Conclusion: Never stop trying to be inclusive

As school leaders we can create an ethos of inclusion through the following simple principles.

Continuous reflection

Learning to learn from our experiences is vital if we want to adapt our leadership and make a difference. We need to think about our approaches as an ongoing system that is flawed but curious to be better. Through continuously reflecting we learn to accept that we often know nothing, but we want to know more. With an issue as complicated as inclusion this approach is invaluable.

Proactive engagement

Do not be afraid to proactively engage in an area where you know or understand little. I have found that seeking the perspectives of those who are too often excluded, as long as I am honest about my ignorance and am curious to learn, has led to some of the greatest lessons I have learnt.

Listening

In leadership there are few better tools in the bag than shutting up and just listening. This is especially true when trying to be more inclusive. When families, young people or children feel listened to and included in the conversation, when they feel that their perspective and experience matters, you go a long way in creating inclusive practice.

Transparency

Making sure everyone has the information they need to understand expectations, the choices they can make and the decisions that you have made is also extremely important when trying to be inclusive.

Accessibility

Our understanding of accessibility needs to be extensive, recognising that our language, environment, curriculum, teaching and leadership style all have an impact on students' sense of safety and inclusion.

Accountability

As leaders of schools, we are accountable to children, young people and families at all times. I believe this accountability runs beyond the barriers of our school. They are national. We can often be detached from the consequences of our decisions because we are just following the rules, but feeling accountable helps us to set the right rules, for the right reasons. I find this is especially true when the challenges are hardest. I have learnt many lessons after permanent exclusions that make me realise leaders still have a role to play and a duty to find the right support for the children and young people we work with. I cannot always be there, but through being a chair of governors in a PRU, for example, I have learnt more about what can be done to support children and young adults than I would ever have by not stepping forward into the role. Through actively engaging with the process beyond mainstream education I have been able to ensure I am developing my knowledge and understanding of an inclusive ethos.

There is so much to learn about leading inclusive schools, and during a long career in education, I still believe I have much more to learn and understand about inclusion, diversity and equity. What I do know, though, is that every school leader needs to acknowledge the challenges they are facing. Post-pandemic I believe we are working in a new era in education where schools are under increasing pressure to deal with increasingly complex problems. Developing our understanding of what effective inclusive practice is will be key in overcoming these challenges in the coming years.

References

Cho, J. H. (2016) 'Diversity is being invited to the party; inclusion is being asked to dance', Verna Myers tells Cleveland Bar (last updated 27.05.16). Available at: www.cleveland.com/business/index.ssf/2016/05/diversity_is_being_invited_to.html [accessed 01.11.22].

Department for Education (DfE) (2020a) Headteachers' standards 2020. Available at: www.gov.uk/government/publications/national-standards-of-excellence-for-headteachers [accessed 28.10.22].

Department for Education (DfE) (2020b) SEND code of practice: 0 to 25 years. Available at: www.gov.uk/government/publications/send-code-of-practice-0-to-25 [accessed 28.10.22].

Eddo-Lodge, R. (2014) Why I am no longer talking to white people about race. Available at: http://renieddolodge.co.uk/why-im-no-longer-talking-to-white-people-about-race [accessed 01.11.22].

McGarvey, D. (2017) *Poverty Safari: Understanding the Anger of Britain's Underclass*. Edinburgh: Luath Press.

5
On Teams

This chapter will explore:

- The need to build an effective team that can successfully adapt to changing educational and local context and challenge
- The key obstacles that stop teams being effective and can cause additional pressure
- The importance of leadership behaviour and the significant impact this can have on the operational vision of a school

---

Introduction

Senior leadership teams have a huge impact on almost every facet of a school and its community. The behaviours, strategy and ambitions displayed within the team create and shape the culture across the school landscape and therefore are the key driver of the outcomes we strive for. How we go about developing our senior team is pivotal to the true success or failure of our school leadership. Whenever I have gone in to support schools in challenging circumstances I have often found that the relationships and behaviours of the senior team give me the greatest insight into what needs to be addressed to make improvements. Getting the team to work well is critical in the journey every school needs to make, no matter where it is in its development. However, when the team is not functioning effectively you can almost guarantee that it will create additional challenges and potentially lead a school into chaos and decline.

Team Team Team

There are a number of senior teams in schools. The SLT (senior leadership team), depending on the size and organisation of your school, is usually made up of teachers leading key areas such as early years, a key stage, departments, critical subjects such as English and maths, or areas such as SEND. Sometimes they might not be class-based, but in my experience, most SLTs have a majority of class-based leaders. This has strengths and limits when it comes to senior leadership which will be discussed in this chapter. At my current school, which has over 100 staff, I have an additional leadership team that sits above the SLT called the ELT (executive leadership team); this small team of four (head teacher, deputy head teacher, assistant head and business manager) focuses on safeguarding, systems, organisation (HR, staffing and so on) and finance. My reason for this is simple: I need my SLT to focus on teaching and learning and not get distracted by other critical areas of school management and leadership. I would also include governors or trustees in this section on senior leaders but again, this will differ by organisation depending on your school context. All headteachers will ultimately be accountable to an executive body (a CEO, or board of trustees). A wise head needs to see them as part of their extended team and draw on their expertise and knowledge.

Behaviour and task

The first and most important rules when thinking about your team follow.

Behaviour matters

The behaviour within any senior leadership teams sets the standards for every-one else. It cultivates the behaviour around it and therefore *what we say, what we do* and *how we do it* really do matter. It is critical that we understand this from the very beginning and strive to make efforts to get it right at all times, because if we don't, we are left trying to repair a broken team and culture which is so much harder to do.

When developing my senior leadership team my first priority is to ensure that our behaviour is right for the job we need to accomplish. I think about this on a number of levels, in the short term, in the long term and based on the remit of the leadership team. I have had to adjust my own behaviour and that of my team on many occasions due to the different contexts and challenges that we have found ourselves working in. The first element in doing this is getting a good understanding of the nature of the challenge ahead, the con-text we are in and what targets we can achieve in the short term (often easy wins) and the longer term (maintaining our focus). Some tasks are suited for SLTs whereas others may be better for other teams such as governors to tackle. Thinking about the task and the appropriate team to complete it is worth spending some time on and should not be taken for granted.

For example, if the teaching and learning of mathematics needs to improve it is wholly unlikely that tasking your governors with a critical operational role within this improvement is going to be effective. Governors need to have a strategic overview, knowing the strengths and gaps, but they are rarely expert enough to walk into a classroom and make critical observations that will take things forward – and even if they could, it would not be appropriate. In con-trast, trawling through a deficit budget forecast while facing rising energy costs is a core duty for governors, while spending hours at an SLT meeting looking at the cost of books and pencils would be ineffective use of the time of teaching and learning experts.

Book of legends

I have often wondered why school leaders and their teams end up doing uneth-ical things, or losing their focus. The nature of the job lends itself to an altruistic approach – in fact many people would say that this is one of the reasons it is the 'best job in the world', that we get a sense of doing something special with our lives through helping others to have an education that will develop them and secure their future. There are few things better than bumping into an ex-pupil or colleague who remembers you and what you did for them.

I once met an ex-pupil in the street.

'Sir!' he called out, 'Mr Walton!' I turned to see a 6ft something, tattooed, muscle machine (the spitting image of his dad) bearing down on me. I had that moment where I braced for the uncertain. He had a tough time at school with me. I had been his teacher for two years and there were a number of break-time detentions, discipline meetings with his father, a fixed-term exclusion … a million lectures. As he got nearer, he opened his arms and moved in for a crushing bear hug.

'Book of legends' he said, 'You sir, are in the book of legends!'

After a brief conversation about his life now and listening to his pride in his achievements and how he wanted me to meet his wife and children, I walked away from that encounter a little dazed but feeling like I was walking on air.

Here is my point. In our roles within education, we leave behind a legacy, a mark. Our actions and behaviour today help carve out that future and the future behaviours of the children and people we work with. These actions might seem like they go unnoticed, and mostly they probably do. We may not hear ex-students, ex-teachers (or even parents) scribbling our names into the Book of Legends. However, if we are true to our moral principles we can be pretty certain that someone, somewhere will be remembering us for all the right reasons. That is a mighty fine legacy to have in a profession about education.

And yet there are many examples of school leaders and their teams doing the wrong things, morally and professionally.

I once saw a head teacher dragging another teacher down the corridor. I just stood there dumbfounded as they went past and I watched the head teacher kick the teacher out of the main entrance door. They felt they had a justified reason for doing this, but it cannot be stressed enough to any school leader that the behaviour we show is about the dignity we have as a leader. This dignity is critical. We can sometimes stumble into getting things wrong and not realise until it is too late, but we must always check our behaviour along the path and think about our own moral code and its importance to our role within social justice, human rights and professional integrity. Our moral code may be all we have in times of challenge where we do not know the immediate answers needed for complex problems. Our day-to-day behaviour during these times is critical, and we need to ensure we model it to everyone in our immediate team as well so that we set the example expected. If the leader strays then we make it OK for other senior leaders to act the same way. This can quickly create a very toxic culture in a school.

There are too many teacher and staff tales about senior leaders and senior teams whose behaviour drags educational leadership into the gutter.

What is evident is that with the power and responsibility that senior leadership teams have there is also the possibility to harm and intimidate those who feel disempowered; for example, ignoring the bullying behaviour of colleagues in the name of getting the job done. Some leaders do not have all the tools needed for the role, and when words such as 'poor standards', 'poor teaching' or 'underachievement' are used, there is only one way to solve them: 'their way or the highway'. What years of successful school leadership have taught me is that almost everyone can improve given strong, fair, clear and compassionate support where there are gaps, support that understands the issues and builds upon the member of staff's strengths. Even when the challenge and context are time pressured and seem critical, I have found that compassion, structure and support regularly work in the longer term.

Even when senior leaders do the right thing, there is a blurring between a good school and a culture of fear, intimidation or bullying. At all times, we should fight against this view of the school leader as a bully and actively seek to ensure it does not exist in our leadership behaviour, especially when we face our greatest tests and are under intense pressure. Checking our body language when a parent shouts at us publicly or getting another member of staff to read our email replies for tone and content is helpful, but deep down we need to walk the walk of someone who is rational, calm and composed at the trickiest of times. I consciously ask myself, how do I look (I am not being vain!) when I am riding the storm? Having an idea of how you are coming across and the type of approach you need for the problem you are trying to overcome is always worth some time to think through before it happens, and knowing that you are in control during the moment is a vitally important aspect of leadership. Am I calm – am I in control? If we can see this in ourselves it really helps to support our teams when they are not feeling calm, rational or in control.

Guiding principles for teams

During my career I have developed some guiding principles for what I see as effective school leadership for a team.

The overarching principle has always been to see the whole school as a team – that everyone knows and understands their role within the bigger picture of the organisation. It is the school leader's role to make this happen and understand how the many different teams function as a whole.

Purpose

Education is full of amplification, a dictionary of hyperbole where we aim for 'world-class' or 'world-beating' education systems. These aspirations are admirable but they can easily cloud our focus and set us off into dreaming rather than achieving. It is action that counts when making our schools effective. Having a vision and an ambition is important but make them ones that you can achieve and will make your school better. Every year I write a statement or word on my board in my office. In the past they have been 'focus' or 'challenge'. They set my personal mindset on our purpose for the year and are usually a reminder of what I need to work on, or where I have felt lacking in the past. Having these simple reminders visually in front of me every time I walk into my office helps me to keep focused on the core purpose we have in our role as a school leader. The simpler the statement, I find, the quicker my understanding when I am losing that purpose.

Time

We need to create time to do the important things that need doing. A good school leader needs to be able to warp and bend time so that all of the component parts of the school machine can be oiled at the right time and in the right order. We do this by being very critical of how we spend our time and how our team is spending their time. This could work by cutting a meeting short if there is no outcome or direction, or phoning a person rather than emailing if it looks more like an essay than a response. I see teams get caught up in a vortex of emails when a quick conversation for clarity or reassurance is usually enough. Trying to unpick emails can lose you so much time and focus when a face-to-face conversation can get things back on track and reaffirm why we are doing what we are doing. Checking our position in time is a vital skill to develop and to develop in others. This often needs a personal leadership touch rather than a lofty email response.

Lists

I wrote about lists in Chapter 1, 'On Leadershit', but wanted to expand my thinking a little here in terms of working with teams.

I now revel in list making. I have tried a thousand ways to do it: from the Eisenhower Matrix and SWOT analysis approach to plain old daily top-to-bottom lists. I now pretty much have at least one list on the go at all times. As I have mentioned, I have a whiteboard in my office that I set up yearly sectioned into three columns: 'to do', 'in progress' and 'done'. I then write out the targets, statements and objectives on post-it notes or, if they are major improvement priorities, I write them in red marker pen in the 'to do' column. I make sure I have quick wins in there as well as bigger school development priorities.

I am often just as happy moving something from 'to do' to 'in progress' as I am completing it. When things do not seem to move as they should I meet my team and go through the board, referencing the areas we need to focus on or reflecting on how much progress we have made in other areas. I prefer this method to long School Development Plans, which are lost in a folder on the hard drive, or aren't out and visual all the time. My whiteboard is there every morning when I bring a coffee into my office. It is a constant listed reminder of what we are trying to do.

Visibility

There is nothing worse than leaders who go missing. Everyone notices it, children, parents and staff. We cannot always be on the gates at the start or the end of the day but when we can we should. Being visible makes a huge difference to how we are regarded by our community. I take almost daily walks around my local estate at lunchtime, to get some fresh air and a mental break, but also to be seen in my local community. This visibility is hardest when you are under pressure, or making an unpopular decision within the community, but this is the time to be more visible than ever, to physically drag ourselves into the community and stand up to be counted. To do this as a team can feel empowering. Having my colleagues next to me when difficult decisions are being taken really does help during those more challenging times. Having a team that are seen by the community, during parents evenings, Christmas performances, the start and the end of the day, and meetings with teachers or the PFSA, really matters because it sends the message that you matter to us (the school). It also sends the message to staff that they matter to us as well.

Balance

Ensuring that you create opportunities for balance between work and home is another critical aspect of creating an effective team. There are many factors of stress in school leadership and they can creep up on you very quickly. Raising awareness of your own balance, for example how you use your time, when you leave school, what you take home with you, your sleeping patterns, as well as that of your team, is a very important area to address. I rarely, if ever, take work home with me now – though I cannot lie and say I did not in the first year of all my headships. I do not arrive super early or leave super late unless I have to; I do not see this as a competition between myself and other leaders. If my planned work is on track, I go home. You can invest your life in school and still feel like you have not achieved what you wanted to achieve, therefore it is important to focus on the tasks that need doing while at work. I work effectively to achieve balance through dumping anything that will not achieve a goal or target we have. I have become brutal about this because I have realised you have to be if you want to keep being a school leader. There are far too many distractions and pointless tasks you could do and only realise after that you have wasted precious time on them. I really think hard about why I am doing anything when in school. Expand this out towards your team and ask 'What are we doing that really makes a difference?'. I now know that I have to get my team to think this way as well. When you have one stressed workaholic in your team it can create more problems and issues and upset the balance of the team.

On my journey home, I try to forget about school and think about my personal life. I play music loud in the car, think about what I will do that evening – the food I will be eating, the TV I will watch. I actively try to forget about the baggage of the day. The baggage won't go away, and on top of this there is probably little I can actively do at 5:30pm that will have the impact I want. It is never easy putting work to one side and I can't always do it. For example, I will sometimes drive and then stop on the way home and not drive any further until I have processed the 'school stuff'. Getting this balance right is key to having a long career in education. Getting your team to be able to do it as well is vital if you want an effective team that can continue to function under pressure. Learning to worry less about what you have little control over when at home is a practised skill that takes time to get right, especially at the toughest times.

Kindness

Kindness is not a weakness, it is a strength. This does not mean that we always do what other people want; that is impossible when you work with so many people. However, we can do things in a way that shows empathy, clarity and an honesty that reflects the situation we find ourselves in. I have always seen this as a kindness.

I often imagine that in any given situation where I feel my leadership being tested and my behaviour is under intense scrutiny that I have a remote control that can switch to the channel needed for the situation. An ill-tempered governors' meeting: the calm and clarity channel; an upset member of staff: the empathy and next step channel; an Ofsted inspector on the prowl: the assured and evidence-based channel. This helps set my mind on thinking carefully about the behaviours I am displaying and the actions I need to take. You do not want to get the wrong frequency – trying to be light-hearted when a member of staff discloses marital struggles being a very good example. Your remote control needs to be powered by strong emotional intelligence. Another factor is how we can sometimes press harder on the buttons hoping to find the right channel, completely unaware that the batteries are exhausted. As a school leader, our behaviour is driven from within and we need to understand that changing to meet the various demands means we also need to have the inner reserves to do this. There is nothing harder than showing compassion and understanding to a member of staff who is worried about their health when at the same time your own father is critically unwell in hospital. The truth is, no one wants to see the leader vulnerable. They expect you to be able to adjust, listen and offer advice at all times. However, as much as we adapt to others, our own behaviour needs to be stable and secure. I find that making kindness my default checking point helps me to approach almost every interaction with a positive outlook, even when the message I am delivering is not what the other person wants.

Ofsted wants

I have not included a chapter on the dreaded Ofsted but it has crept into many parts of this book because it is an inescapable factor in school leadership. The most successful schools I have either worked with or visited make no excuses about their approach. They know what they do and why they do it and no one is going to sway this approach. As one very successful head teacher in a very challenging context once told me, 'I don't give a toss about Ofsted and nor do my team'. This is a good philosophy to have about Ofsted.

I have led through many inspections over my years as a school leader and been lucky enough (as of the time of writing this book) to never have had a bad one – although I have worked in many schools after they have and fully understand why, as much as Ofsted should not matter, it does. The problem with Ofsted is people constantly try to second-guess them. They look to crack the formula, especially if they are under pressure or increased scrutiny, rather than keeping to their principles, understanding and experience of what good practice in 'their' school needs to look like. When we do this, we limit ourselves to running a school within a perceived ideology of what that success looks like. I am still waiting to walk into a school that is the same as any other school I have been into – they just do not exist. Since 1995, when I became a teacher, the expectations and system of Ofsted have constantly changed along with Department for Education expectations. Trying to have a long-term strategy based on what a top-down country-wide system wants is not going to work in a day-to-day way, and what happens is we find schools flitting from one approach, scheme or system to another and never truly allowing practice to embed. It is often teams that drive this imbalance because they have competing priorities within their day-to-day role within the team and this is quite often fuelled by fear, especially as the Ofsted inspection date approaches and looms large in the calendar.

I have lost count over the years of the number of times I have heard people begin a training session, feedback, initiative or more frequently a sales pitch with the line 'Ofsted wants … '. It is 2022 as I write this and schools are awash with new curriculums that have Intent, Implementation and Impact running down their spine. I am not saying that this is not good practice but it took Ofsted to say it for the whole system to do it. These decisions were taken by leadership teams up and down the country, not because this was well-researched fundamental practice but because it is simple, makes sense and when Ofsted comes into the school it gives them a narrative they can communicate to the inspectors. One of the primary roles of the senior team is to know what it is doing and why it is doing it and communicating that across the organisation; if it is set up to save our backsides when Ofsted arrives then it is just a smoke-screen. It takes leaders who know their school and what they are doing to break away from the straitjacket of Ofsted, and when they do you can pretty much guarantee they get it right.

I can vividly recall the moment an Ofsted inspector told my team that we were going to get an Outstanding grade in our inspection. I had been the head teacher at the school for seven years and it felt like the culmination of all those years of hard work from the difficult first inspection, through to Good and now this, an Ofsted Outstanding grade. The affirmation, joy and emotion were overwhelming, for about two days. Big wins in education are rare and Ofsted can feel like a big win or lose situation. This is probably why they drive team strategy and actions so often. It took getting an Outstanding grade to make me realise I really do not care about them. The report became meaningless days after publication and clearly did not reflect the school I, and my team, knew. I wondered – if ten inspectors came in, one after the other, would they all give the same judgement? I doubt it. Therefore, I now see Ofsted as an *unavoidable inconvenience* I have to put myself, and my team, through every five years or so. If I can get through my career without taking a school I lead into a negative category then that would be one less stress to go through. Do I think that is possible? I have no idea because Ofsted is far too erratic and far too unpre-dictable, more so now than at any other time. Therefore, I do not even try to think about what they might do or say when they come in. I just concentrate on what *we* will do and say.

After my school received the Outstanding judgement I quickly felt demoti-vated and realised I loved the old days when we were Good but aspirational to be better. After an Ofsted Outstanding judgement, it very quickly becomes a legacy, and this then supports a system where Outstanding schools do not see another inspection for ten years or more. Teams need to be built around under-standing what they are doing, why they are doing it and what difference they are making. It really is as simple as that, and yet it goes wrong far too often. I have argued for years that Ofsted inspections do not need judgements – they just need to make key recommendations moving forward. At most, either you are doing a good enough job or you are not.

Making progress

Teams have to make progress. When a sense of progress is lacking, teams can quickly become demotivated and unfocused. Progress is a key ingredient in driving teams' actions and behaviours. Progress can boost emotions; it can motivate individual and team ambitions, making them productive and focused on the goal that they want to achieve. If you can ensure that you manage progress well you can develop a team that is driven in a positive way to complete tasks to an effective outcome. Therefore, do not set targets that are too big. Break down goals so that success is driven by a sense of progress towards something needed. Sweat the small stuff, so to speak, and celebrate smaller milestones rather than worry about the fact that you have not perfected assessment across the school. It is likely you never will.

In the longer term we need to think more strategically about our targets and goals. Many of the problems faced by leadership teams fall into a small number of categories:

- Firefighting and safeguarding: Issues that can arise suddenly and unexpectedly or need a longer-term stewardship, which can fall into the crisis management category. This is where the stress of the job can be intense and often involves safeguarding others
- Curriculum school development priorities: Issues that have been identified as gaps in provision that through development can be improved to provide a better service, impacting directly on teaching and learning. This is where Ofsted will focus, and when in challenging circumstances is the area that is hardest to change without significant investment
- Business school development priorities: Issues such as financial constraints, site complications and human resources. Chapter 7 on business covers this in more detail, but basically this needs careful management and can distract your team from teaching and learning if not managed well

In all these areas the team needs to understand its role and what it is trying to achieve. If we know what we are aiming for we have a better collective understanding of how we might get there.

I have spent decades trying to write effective targets that help scaffold my teams through the many challenges we have faced, and I have ended up with a very simple solution: stop overcomplicating things.

Stop overcomplicating things

There is a real tendency in education to make things longer than they need to be, to spend more time on things because we feel that they are not perfect, and we usually write more than we need to. Targets on School Development Plans are so often far too long and complicated. They are assigned to people in complicated ways, they are budgeted in ways that do not exist in the real world, and they are given time limits that seem to be picked out of thin air. I have come to the conclusion that the best thing I can do as a head teacher is to be very clear on what we are trying to achieve in its purest form and how the team can make this happen. For example, if our school is in Special Measures and we know what put us there I would first ask: Why are we doing this? What is better like? What will we do next? I would then ask: What can we control and what is beyond our control?

I ask the same questions when the Ofsted is Good, when a vital member of the team is promoted or leaves, when a new initiative comes in, when we have challenges in behaviour. I ask the simplest questions possible to know if the objectives, targets and actions make sense, move us forward or have a positive impact.

Great teams need great leadership but we often only look at leadership through individuals and we usually only do this retrospectively. I do not believe any of the teams I have worked with would have seen me as a *great* leader (in fact I imagine they would have been amused at the thought). This is because I hope they saw that we were much more nuanced than one person's skill set making everything happen. I have had many challenging and difficult days and weeks trying to develop the senior teams of my school but I now look back at them all and feel a huge sense of pride because of what we achieved collectively and what they became individually. Many are now head teachers and senior leaders in their own schools, and though I miss working with *most* of them, I am proud to have been part of their development journeys. A key component to this was ensuring I understood my team well and gave them space to develop, sometimes at my own cost.

I have three weekly meetings with my senior teams; one with my SLT who are also mostly class-based teachers where we reflect on the weekly diary and teaching and learning, and two meetings with my ELT where we look at operational and safeguarding issues. In all meetings, we go over a fixed agenda. This is where we reflect, review and plan for action. This is the time to strike off issues and acknowledge progress towards a goal. To make sure that this is not lost, every meeting has minutes taken and emailed out to everyone in attendance. The formula is set out and actions shared and stamped completed or pending depending on their status. We go over these actions at the start of every meeting to see what is holding them up, or celebrate/acknowledge their completion.

Building teams

When building an effective team you need to think carefully about how you take an eclectic group of people who are usually very good at performing their own individual goals and tasks within the school and get them to understand and accomplish whole-school objectives with a sense of unity. They need to do this in such a way that they empower those around them and are clinical with their time and focus. Building great teams is far from easy and they often need to develop through a number of phases.

The first thing to remember when creating your senior team is to think long term over two to five years. It is very unlikely as a new school leader that you will have any say in or knowledge about the people you are working with. Unless you are internally promoted (and this brings its own challenges through a change of accountability), you will inherit your team, its history and legacy as well as the myths, facts and baggage surrounding the individuals in your team. In all of my roles as a head teacher there is an unwritten legacy surrounding the past of the teams within a school. It is your job to create an open, honest and transparent team and it is quite likely that you will need to break down key barriers to get to this. That is why I give myself a longer-term vision for what I want from my team. It is quite simple really:

I want the team to be able to have constructive arguments without the fear of conflict or the focus straying away from actions that need to happen.

I want them to scrutinise and critique the weaknesses in our arguments and plans – the classic 'you can disagree with me in the meeting but when we are outside this room, we must all be in agreement'.

I want to have a group of people around me who are not all the same. This is vital but not always achievable. Developing the people on your team to feel comfortable sharing and developing their different perspectives is one of the most challenging parts of managing a team, but in the long term has always been the vital ingredient that has helped me develop my personal goals as well as the objectives and targets within the school. To do this I make sure my teams have strengths and ambitions for the organisation that differ. For example, the business manager prioritises the financial and smooth organisational running of the school. That is what they are paid to do. They need to understand the school's purpose and objectives, but they also need to be brutally honest about the feasibility of plans around the curriculum, staffing and future teaching and learning developments. I always want a pastoral lead on my senior team, someone who looks out for other people. This can often be in direct conflict with business. I always have a Special Educational Needs Coordinator (SENCo) on my team; someone who will often fight tooth and nail regarding inclusion issues. I also want someone with a systemic and operational understanding of teaching, learning and the curriculum. I have never worried about my executive team being the 'best teachers' in school, though I feel that an SLT must have some of the strongest teachers in it. I want my best teachers in the classroom teaching every day without distractions. It is my executive team's goal to make that happen, rather than pretending we were once 'great teachers' and could do what teachers do but are far too busy. You do not become an Olympic champion in swimming by training in judo. I want my team practising how to be a senior team leading a school in all its complexity. This is not to say they do not understand teaching and learning. They 'have to'. They all need to be able to 'walk the walk' and be very visible across the school on a day-to-day basis, but they need to acknowledge the teachers as the experts.

I then make sure I have as many senior leaders trained in safeguarding as possible. I currently have four designated safeguarding leads in my senior team and they all have a specific area of the school and a weekly meeting to discuss cases.

This knowledge and skill base has always helped my schools move forward in a balanced and effective way. Even though the people in the team are very different, their motives vary and their skill sets are not the same, they learn to work together to become an effective team. It is so easy in education to keep doing what we have always done – especially if it works. I like the idea of evolving over time, tweaking and not taking the success we have for granted. It is not about changing everything, there is just too much to do, but you need to understand what needs to change and be brave enough to do something about it. To use sports management as an example, in the past you would often see individual sports managed by experts in their field; people who had only been footballers, ice skaters or athletes. There is a lot of sense in bringing together the expertise someone has gained over years in a given field – but having experts in the same field together can also be an echo chamber of sorts. They might disagree but ultimately their knowledge is expert and often built upon very similar backgrounds and foundations of success and failure. They often grow indoctrinated into the same systems and assumptions. I always wonder what an expert from another field would bring to the SLT table. I once did a leadership training course when I first became a head teacher, and the other participants were leaders in engineering, prison governance, the NHS and social work and a local football manager. I walked away from the training session feeling that we had much in common in terms of the day-to-day challenges but went about managing and leading very differently. The overwhelming challenge was managing people. I still often wonder whether I could run a social work team, football club or prison. How much subject-specific knowledge would I need? I certainly would need some, but the idea I would have to be the expert is flawed given I would have a team of them who I would need to manage effectively. Therefore, I would need to be an expert in organising, motivating and leading effective teams and building a collective trust and goal.

Trust

Trust is the cornerstone of building a team. If you cannot build and protect the trust within your team, then everything else you do will falter. It can be far harder than it would seem because you need to take a group of individuals and make them work together without the fear of being vulnerable. This often takes time and a well-thought-out consistency in your words and actions as you lead the team through this process.

At its heart you need to be able to link the connections within your team together. The easiest connection is that of the purpose of education. Everyone I have ever worked with in education wants to do the best they can for their school. It is just that everyone has different motives, experiences, knowledge bases and skills. How the school leader makes sense of this and allows them to develop and flourish is very important.

At times, I have felt that developing the senior team has been the most challenging part of running an effective school. Building trust can be difficult. As Patrick Lencioni (2002) illustrates in his book *The Five Dysfunctions of a Team*, the absence of trust is the key blocker in effective teamwork because it does not allow people to be vulnerable within the group. This in turn creates fear of conflict. Understanding how we allow constructive conflict in our team is so important but it is also very challenging to manage. Having conflict means we are not all just going through the motions and agreeing with each other. It means we have opposing ideas and ways in which to get to our goals. Allowing the team to voice this without any fear enables the team to function in the longer term much more effectively. Spending time when you are the new school leader addressing this issue with your team and how you are going to be able to have conflict without hurting feelings or creating a false harmony really helps. I have tried many ways – usually starting with a set of principles we need to have that we collectively draw up. I find that in the early stages, revisiting these regularly helps us start meetings with a clear understanding of what we want to achieve as a team. Eventually the team's behaviours should mean that we can have constructive agreement and disagreement without having to refer to the principles, or having anyone storm out of the room.

Setting principles

Within the senior team, we want to promote integrity, respect and responsibility in our actions. From experience, it is not difficult to implement these principles, but we need to go into more detail than this if we are to achieve it. They will vary from school to school and need to reflect the context you find yourself in, but I tend to have no more than six or seven. For example, these are the current principles my team work towards:

1. Ensure each learning encounter is purposeful in order to maintain high levels of enthusiasm and behaviour – we prioritise progress for everyone
2. Constantly reflect on all data, our own practice and professional knowledge in order to set ambitious targets that reflect realistic goals
3. Act with care and compassion, ensuring that all members of the community are treated fairly and impartially
4. Have high expectations of all behaviour in all areas and at all times – all senior leadership staff are responsible for instilling and maintaining this

I will then follow this up with specific expectations within the senior leadership meetings; for example, at our meetings we will:

• Make decisions, share information, consider ideas for improvement, coordinate and review work, challenge prevailing thought and practice, prioritise, resolve conflict and support the work of the Academy.

You could add or take away from this list. At certain times, it may be prudent to just focus on a smaller number of ideas (say in the autumn term, for example, where you may want your meetings to be just about reflecting on data or behaviour).
    We will achieve this through:

• Using evidence and research (school-based as well as from wider sources) to inform our decisions whenever possible
• Listening to and valuing everyone's opinion
• Thinking about the *bigger* picture while representing the views of our teams
• Having clear agendas that focus on a purpose embedded in teaching and learning and the wellbeing of our community (senior staff are expected to add to the agenda at least a day before the meeting)

The final part is making sure the meetings are minuted, specifically for actions so that everyone is in agreement about what they will do after the meeting. The next meeting agenda then starts with these actions. This helps keep senior leadership team meetings focused on the issues at hand, rather than becoming a free-for-all discussion on the current topic of the week.

Conclusion: One team

Even when senior teams believe they are doing the right thing there becomes a blurring between an amazing school and a culture of 'fear, intimidation and bullying'. The school leader needs to be on top of this. Your leadership is the vital ingredient in the effective running of the senior leadership team and this ensures that there is a clear improvement focus in the plans and actions across the school. How you create a team and utilise the skills and knowledge within it to get the best results in the short and long term go a long way to ensuring your time as the school's leader is a productive one. Understanding and navigating through the obstacles that stop teams being effective helps to create a productive and positive culture within the school community, giving you the belief and ability to overcome almost every challenge school leadership can throw at you.

Reference

Lencioni, P. (2002) *The Five Dysfunctions of a Team: A Leadership Fable*, San Francisco, CA: Jossey-Bass.

6

On Leading and Managing Change

This chapter will look at one of the most difficult tasks a leader has: leading and managing change across a school setting. It will look at the following elements:

- How to approach change
- How change provokes a wide range of personal responses that impact on the effectiveness of the process and potentially the outcomes of the changes we want to make
- Developing an understanding of how your approach needs a certain vision, intelligence and flexibility to better understand the what and how of the change purpose
- Understanding the importance of 'getting the balance right' when invoking the change process so that it impacts positively in the long run but does not cause a complete breakdown within school processes or staff wellbeing in the short term
- The three stages of looking at change within a school setting

Introduction

Early in my first headship I introduced a new computerised assessment system across the school because I felt that the paper-based version was onerous, confusing and repetitive. I thought that it didn't give those responsible for improving teaching and learning the necessary overview or detail to make effective decisions so that children could make better progress. Well, that was 'my' argument with myself. You will have noticed that I have used the pronoun *me* here. What I failed to understand at this early stage in my headship was that many staff liked the system because they understood it and they had made it work for the way they taught on a day-to-day basis. At the time of making the change I wasn't concerned about outcomes – our observations and data showed that children were doing well, in fact a few years later the school got an outstanding Ofsted based on consistently good outcomes. I just didn't like the paper version because I felt that it was outdated, and the truth of the matter was I couldn't understand how to make it work as a school leader. I remember a senior member of staff asking to meet with me to talk through my proposals, and as I explained that I understood that change can be scary she looked at me and said, 'I'm not afraid of change Brian, but it had better well work because, as I have seen a hundred times before, we end up with a god-awful mess and go back to the same system we started off with. All it did was waste everyone's precious time'.

In my experience, leading and managing change can be one of the most challenging parts of senior school leadership. I believe that this stems from a number of reasons but most commonly the fact that in education teachers can easily feel overwhelmed by a lack of continuity and empowerment over the area that they have the most knowledge and understanding about – the teaching and the learning taking place in their classroom. When change is implemented it can often be a top-down process in which teachers and school staff are told something needs to change and they are given little say in what happens next – therefore, the very mention of change brings fear and dread because it also brings a sense of powerlessness.

There was a lot to learn from my first negative encounter with making whole - school change, most importantly really understanding the *why* of the change that we were making and the impact it would have on processes, systems and people. Digging deep and ensuring that everyone could see the reason for the initial upheaval and, as a leader and school staff, understanding why it needed to happen in the first place was crucial – most importantly unpicking the *why*, as leader, the decision for change was the right one. The key lesson I have learnt from this process and one I practise to this day is: *Can I explain the reason for the change in a few simple sentences?*

Heard it all before

When you introduce a change into the School Development Plan you are almost certainly going to get a broad spectrum of reactions to it. I heard many of these phrases as a teacher and I still hear them today after more than 19 years of leading schools as a head teacher:

- Why are we changing this?
- What are we changing this for and how is it better?
- How is this going to impact on me and my role within the school?
- What are we *not* going to do now so that we can do this *new* extra thing?
- I can't see how this is going to work
- It's OK for them to ask for the change – they don't have to do it!
- This is 'top-down' policy but useless in the classroom
- I have seen it all before, it's what we did a decade ago. It will not last
- At last, it is about time we changed this! (Quite rare this one)

For the school leader making changes you are very likely to hear these or very similar phrases from teachers, governors, parents and children. You are also going to invoke a range of emotions towards the change, and sometimes this is shown as frustration, confusion or even anger and can lead to conflict within your team. Therefore, a critical thing to have in mind before you make changes that will impact systems and processes is a clear plan laying out your methods – especially for the early stages – and a rigorously and carefully scheduled communication process that outlines the needs of the organisation within the change process. This can take time and research, but I would say that the bigger the change the more time you need to think before you act.

Don't get carried away

It is easy for a leader introducing change to get excited. We may have been at a conference where someone tells their story of change and we want to bring this vibrant and exciting thing to our school. In the conference hall, full of atmosphere, vibrant slides and a passionate advocate who is sharing a retrospective that may have taken years or even decades, it is so easy to buy into the change and on Monday morning scrap the weekly senior leadership team agenda to try to convince colleagues (who weren't there) that this is the future – the new dawn that will solve all those problems we have been struggling with for months. It is so easy to fall into the trap of change, an invitation to a better school and a better way of doing things. If only it was that simple. I remember the first time I read about School 21 where assemblies are used to really empower children's learning and parent's evenings are run by the children – I wanted my school to be like that. How hard could it be to implement these changes into the system? The brutal truth is you cannot make changes that radically alter the culture, system and vision of your school overnight; it takes years. You have to have this voice in the back of your head at all times saying, 'Slow down and think this through'.

Daydreamer

For change to be successful you need to be able to see a clear path through the process you are about to start. You need to know what kind of change you are creating and how each stage is going to play out. I spend a lot of time daydreaming. I have daydreamed moments of success and challenge a thousand times during my career. Everything from successful Ofsted outcomes, to new builds, expansions of provision, what a successful Special School looks like on a mainstream site. Visualising what I want, what it would feel like, look like and sound like helps me in this early stage. I really believe there is nothing wrong with senior leaders spending time dreaming. I often plan change in three stages, and when spending time visualising what it is I want to achieve I go through each stage in my mind.

Stage 1: Why and what

What is the point?

There needs to be a clear and compelling case for the change to happen. There is a world of difference between a school going into Special Measures and a school wanting to develop their marking policy because they feel it does not allow for enough pupil voice. Understanding the urgency for the change has much to do with how the process will develop. What sort of change is required? Gradual or radical? It could be argued that gradual change rarely needs a major plan, that this slow changing of processes is part of the normal cycle of school development. At best, this change needs to be on a School Development Plan but it may just be an agenda item on a senior leadership team meeting or a series of staff meetings. It is when change is more radical and far reaching and has a wider impact that we need to carefully plan for it.

The change process you are invoking should be in the School Development Plan (or whatever you call it – I tend to use Academy Development Plan but do not overthink Development or Improvement – it's a plan to move things forward). If the change is going to have a school-wide impact, it really needs good evidence. Leaders need to clearly and simply communicate what this means to everyone involved and find a way to show this:

- Why we need to do this
- What this will mean to you on a day-to-day basis
- The impact we hope this will have on children, staff and the school as a whole

Lost in translation

Every act of communication is also a reflection on translation. There is a very important thing to understand when making change you absolutely feel is vital. You need to see it in a positive light and make others also see this light and feel its positive glow. If you cannot see that light, trust me when I say leading others to it will be very hard. Spending time as a leader really understanding the nuances of the change you need to make and communicating this to others is critical in the early stages. This cannot be some sort of blind rallying cry that ignores the problems – in fact it must be the opposite: a warts-and-all synopsis of the change needed and why it is still the best thing we can do. It is important to remember that everything that you change was likely part of a past change process. Remember, everyone wants to get something out of this change. What motivates your staff to embrace any change you make is critical insider information – ask them, be honest. Is it for an easier life, better outcomes for children, less hours at work? Your change may well be the best thing in education since the pencil, but if your staff are working three more hours a week because of it, it may not be worth it in the end.

If only asking staff what they want was that simple though. You ask them and they tell you and we all live happily ever after. Many people want a safe and secure profession. They like knowing where they stand and what their role is within the grand scheme of things. This gives them security – sometimes it is a false security because that safety is negatively impacting on their own well-being, effectiveness or future role in the school because they see it as normal, what they have always done and they don't even know it. But, and this is a very big but, I have also made changes many times believing I was doing the best thing in the world only to realise after the change that what we did before was better, and having to admit that to staff after a world of upheaval and unhappiness is not only a very difficult and uncomfortable process but can also be very damaging for staff morale in the long run. Therefore, the more honest we are about the challenges we will face making the change, the better.

Well ... Ofsted

Another mistake we can make when communicating with staff about why we are making a change (and I still make this mistake) is to allude to, or directly say, 'Well ... Ofsted'. From most teachers' perspectives, this gaming of the system – doing things based on what we have heard, or feel, Ofsted will want when they inspect – sits uncomfortably and will often provoke negative feelings and comments. It also plays on anxiety and fear and quite often further feeds that panic about Ofsted. We do need to be careful here though; by its very nature, Ofsted's focus will have much in common with the priorities within most of our schools. Whether we like it or not they influence and impact on key aspects of policy and structure within our education system. However, it is a lazy leader who uses them as the stick to get their staff to change. When change comes about, 'Ofsted wants' is a poor substitute for motivating the teachers and staff in classrooms working with children on a day-to-day basis to work harder and change their practice. Ofsted is often a strategic movement in education – big overarching themes such as the curriculum, safeguarding, teaching, learning and assessment. When we make changes in our school and lose the context through pointing towards some faceless inspectorate we really risk alienating our school community. Raising the spectre of the Ofsted Bogeyman has never, in my experience, worked for positive change. It is a dangerous gamble that adds additional complexities to the process. Making fear the driver for change must be avoided if we want sustainable change, and therefore 'Ofsted wants' in change management must become '*We* need to change this *because*'.

Data love/data hate

I *love* data. I could spend hours and hours looking at it and trying to work out what it could be telling me, or more commonly, what it does not tell me. Data is the friend and the enemy of most school leaders. It can be dangerous in the wrong hands and if not used sensitively it can set you on the wrong course and it could be a long time before you realise this. Therefore, when making changes I spend a lot of time trying to work out what data we have, and what I think – and others think – this data tells us about why we need to act and make a change, or vitally on occasions do nothing.

Statistical data is usually pretty easy to understand. 'Only 30 percent of our Pupil Premium children are at age-related expectations in Year 3', for example, would be a good starting point at which to ask what change is required to make a positive difference to this. By its very nature though, we need to look further, and so often I have seen leaders set out ambitious whole-school change plans based on data only to realise that we are effectively looking at six children across two year groups. OK, six very important children, but why are we making changes across the entire school to address cohort-specific issues? I have seen so many misunderstandings of data in which the school has made fundamental work practice change only to find out the issue needed to be addressed on a much more targeted and individual basis.

My first rule when looking at data is that it is most likely flawed and inaccurate, so be careful. The number of times I have used data in a positive and negative light only to realise it was all rubbish are too numerous to mention (around 53.5%, or something). Therefore, we have to be extra careful with it. For example, I have heard school governors ask: '82 percent were at age-related expectations in reading at Year 2 last year; why are only 71 percent of our Year 2 children this year at age-related expectations in reading – what are we doing about it? Have standards dropped?'

'Err, it's different children. A different cohort. There are 8 percent more children with SEND.'

The important thing is not always the data but the context around the data. For me this is the thing we need to know and understand when making the change, not necessarily the numbers. The best thing we can do is humanise the data through context and narrative. Get our intelligence right; know the detail well before we blunder into the implementation phase.

Stage 2: Making it happen

Implementing the changes

The implementation process is very important and needs to be sensitively managed. It is very likely to have many obstacles and problems to overcome and setting it up without acknowledging the difficulties ahead can often be a recipe for disaster. A good approach to setting the implementation up is to think: What will it take for this to fail?

I often think and plan to fail because it helps to reflect on the possible problems that could be faced at this crucial implementation phase. I think about what could happen when teachers feel alone and up against the challenges of the change and leaders are no longer in the blue sky safety zone of planning for a better outcome.

Plan to fail

Implementation requires us to visualise what the success looks like. It is important to know what success will be like and how we can celebrate this success. I find that by also visualising the barriers and the reason why something fails I have a head start in planning for future success. When planning to fail we can be very specific. If we think a change will fail because we don't have the money for the resources to make the transition, then going ahead without those resources is pointless unless we can either find another way to finance it, or we don't make the change we originally said we would.

There are a lot of reasons why a change initiative will fail. I have listed some of the most common ones I have faced during my time trying to lead successful change.

Leaders losing sight of what they intended

When we plan for change it is usually a blue sky thinking moment. It is free and easy to say 'let's do this, move that, make these resources, tell them this', but the reality is, once that change has been planned and agreed upon you need a different type of approach. You need to see the implementation through and this can be far from exciting; it may even be a little bit dull and boring. Whatever it is, it will need good management skills, perseverance and an awareness of the possible pitfalls, such as:

- Leaders and managers who become inactive or invisible
- Leaders who set expectations that are either too high or not high enough
- Leaders who do not address wavering commitment
- Leaders who do not manage a developing lack of accountability. This is especially damaging when this comes from middle leaders who have not bought into the change, have not had a chance to voice their concerns to leaders and therefore voice their concerns to staff
- Leaders who fail to see competing objectives which then become seen as more important, or confuse staff with too many competing changes and challenges
- Leaders who become or create gatekeepers – people who have all the keys, skills and knowledge to make the change effective who, for a variety of reasons, do not share this information and therefore the change is utterly reliant on them. Lose the gatekeeper and lose access to the planned changes. I spend quite a bit of time trying not to make my change process reliant on one person – especially me

- Leaders who fail to manage roles which become confused or disappear altogether
- Leaders who fail to manage the resistance

La Résistance

If the very *idea* of change was met with resistance, it is quite likely that the disruption to routines and set ways of doing things during the implementation phase *will* be met by even stronger opposition. Change in practice will often increase resistance for many reasons, such as the change isn't seen quickly enough or happens too quickly, or because it needs time to embed, or things get more challenging for staff in the initial phases of the change. In fact, there is always a possibility that the implementation process will grow a culture of resistance because staff experiences are not what they expected, and they can evidence why things are *not* working in the real world and why it was better in the good old days before the change.

I dislike the often quoted '20% will be resistant, 60% open and 20% will be active participants in the change idea'; it depends on what you are trying to change and why. I think what is worth understanding in the implementation is some staff will be actively helping the change take place and some will not. I have never come across a situation in which *everyone* is resistant; I think if I did, I would look towards doing something else, or find a new career! You need to go into change with a majority of people seeing and believing in the change and in agreement that the change is at least a good idea. To make it work though you need to make sure that those who are sitting on the fence do not fall off onto the wrong side and become part of the resistance. You do not want to lose them. Managing the resistance is about facing up to it and trying to understand why it is there in operation, and the best way to do this is to watch it in practice. This can, of course, cause even further issues because the staff who are resistant and feel it doesn't work will not be lining up for a lesson observation, a report or a walkthrough on the thing that they hate and want rid of. Therefore, we have to make sure that we addressed the monitoring of the implementation in stage 1, and make sure that the stakes for learning about the impact at this stage are not about beating people with sticks but learning from the experiences that they have. Too often leaders are detached from the realities of teachers and teaching assistants – we have a vision for what we want and do not understand why it cannot work because we are far too detached from it. By observing the change, being openly critical of how you are implementing it and why it is a challenge or just isn't working, in practice goes a long way in understanding the barriers the staff have in the change process and making adjustments to help the implementation. This may mean making compromises, but that is better than a complete breakdown.

Sink or swim – make capacity your number one priority

Capacity is possibly the most important factor when implementing change. You need to plan for it and you need to sustain it through the implementation of the change process. Capacity is about understanding how the resources you have available interact to accommodate successful change. An assistant head I once worked with, who is now a head teacher, talked about our capacity as a vehicular chain ferry such as the King Harry Ferry which crosses the estuary of the River Fal in Cornwall. It has a capacity of 34 cars. That means we know exactly how many cars we can successfully transport across the river, but what happens if you take two lorries? Our capacity is the same but the number of cars changes. Therefore, if you know and understand your capacity at the start you can adjust the ways in which you implement the change. The original capacity we have and the load placed on it will dictate whether you can make the change a successful one or not. Overload and it's likely the change process, like the ferry, will sink; underload and you may be wasting resources on something that does not have the impact you originally thought it would.

When we look at the resources needed for change there are a few important factors to remember:

- People
- Time
- Money

I'm only human

As I set out in Chapter 7, 'On Finance and Business', people are the greatest resource a school leader has; more than money, time or space I have found that people are the crucial factor in successful whole-school change in the places I have worked. This is why recruitment and retention are among the key areas that cause head teachers the most stress within the role. Come March to May every year the ins and outs within a school are about our capacity to deliver in the future. In fact, I would now go as far as saying recruitment for some schools is an all-year-round worry. However, March to May is when we usually find out if we are to lose a teacher and will need to bring in those starting out on their career, changing school or taking on a subject or leadership role for the first time. This human element needs to be understood alongside the changes we intend to implement. If we do not have the right people in place to deliver, then not only is the change likely to fail, it may also cause further problems within the current system that have a negative knock-on impact on other areas. Therefore, I really try not to plan any real change until I have as secure a picture of my staffing as I can have, usually around June or July. This can be late if looking at September implementation but it is better than setting something up that we cannot staff or do not have the skills to see through.

To praise, or not to praise

We have looked at the drivers needed to get buy-in to change. This is critical at the beginning and continues to need good leadership and management throughout the implementation phase. People need to feel listened to, feel that they can feed back into the process and have their hard work and contributions acknowledged and celebrated at the right times.

The least anyone wants, in my experience, is acknowledgement for what they have done; a recognition that they are doing their best under the circumstances they are in. Celebrating any success within the change process is different for different people though – some people like to be praised, privately or publicly, some hate this, some like acknowledgement for their hard work, others feel uncomfortable with this and see it as them 'just doing their job'. There are those who need extra time, money and/or responsibility to feel that they have been fairly treated in the process. Knowing and understanding the different motives the people you work with have can help in ensuring that you keep the people you need fully focused on the change. In the past, I have asked staff how they want their contributions to be celebrated. The worst I can do is say 'That is not possible', the best is to accommodate the request. Either way, we all know and understand where we are within the process. This way you have a better idea of what to do or not to do when things are going well or are not. The least I expect of my staff is that we develop an ethos where talking about what is going well or not going well is encouraged and carefully handled.

Time – the Pomodoro technique

I am a strong believer that many people in education find the effective use of time a real struggle. Time is vital where there can be a hundred distractions and emergencies that stop you focusing on the strategic elements of the job. Time is so important but often we do not give it the respect it deserves. Using time effectively and with focus is something I have always needed to work hard at. That is why I have found the Pomodoro technique really useful throughout my time as a school leader.

The Pomodoro technique was developed by Francesco Cirillo, who found he struggled to stay focused on his studies and completing assignments. He found that if he committed to short spaces of time – including setting a timer (which was shaped like the *pomodoro* – 'tomato' in Italian) – and staying focused on that given task until the timer rang he would become more productive. Time is often about managing all the distractions that stop you doing the task you need to complete. Leadershit is the nemesis of time, sucking it into a void, and therefore, through controlling our time, we can also filter out what is worthwhile and what is not. Giving your absolute attention to a task, even for small amounts of time, can be an incredibly effective way of making progress on it. I used this technique to finish this book while still leading a school full time – small, focused sessions writing with absolute focus.

Initially you need to make sure you have broken the task down into achievable chunks. You will not be able to achieve teaching and learning Nirvana across your school in 20 minutes – but you could attempt to write the introduction to the policy. Time management is also about knowing what you want to achieve.

Set your timer for 20 minutes and focus on a single task until the timer rings.

Then take a small break, have a cup of tea, go for a short walk around school if you are doing this task while at school. Then come back and review what you have achieved. If you need to do more and have deadlines, set the timer again.

Time is everything for the school leader, a precious resource that we need to understand and get right. You know when you have got it right and that is usually when you no longer find yourself writing your Self Evaluation Plan on a Sunday afternoon. If you find you are making progress on key actions and not working very late or at the weekends, it is very possible you are managing your time and focus well.

I practise leaving work before 5pm every day. I am not bad at it. There are days when I go way past this but there are many days when I do not. I will only leave if I know I am on top of priorities. I will not take work home unless I absolutely have to. I rarely, if ever, work on the weekend anymore. This has taken me a long time to get right but I feel no different about workload than I did when I used to work past 6pm every day and spent Sunday updating my School Development Priorities. The only difference is I now plan my time more effectively than I did and I care less about the fluff within the job and much more about the things that really matter.

Money – the cost of change

I have written a chapter about the importance of understanding our budgets in school leadership, but within a specific change project, there are a few things to consider because the success or failure of the change you want to bring about can live or die on the blade of the budget.

It is important to understand the cumulative costs of change management because many change projects worth taking time to plan for are about longer-term changes. When change is over time there are often many hidden costs that no matter how well you plan for will unexpectedly crop up. Think of it like house renovation and as the floorboards come up you realise that you have dry rot in the foundations. You may have considered this in the 'planning to fail' stage, but if your worst fears are realised it may be that money becomes the biggest factor as to whether successful change can continue, or even take place.

The major factors to consider regarding budget within a change management process are the following:

- Training – good CPD can be done in many ways but there are some that will need specialist help and specific support. This can be costly and may need to be done over a longer period to manage the impact that it will have on time within the daily structure of the school. Staff cannot become experts in one session and there is a big difference to fire evacuation drill training and many aspects of developing teaching and learning processes and systems. Some training will have an ongoing yearly cost – factor this in
- Resources – some change needs little additional resource apart from people, time and a will to do it. On other occasions, a resourcing budget can have ongoing costs. This is spectacularly true with elements of computing infrastructure or buying consultancy time to help project manage change. Laying out the resources you need and the costs before you press the button to make the change happen can be one of the wisest moves you make
- Restructuring – for example, redundancy payments to staff. It is better to know this before you do the restructure

In your reflections, measuring the costs accurately may allow you to find ways to reduce or entirely avoid certain costs. Sometimes I have ignored the rising costs, and on reflection, I have seen mistakes where I wasted money on something that in retrospect had little impact on the change and could have easily been avoided. I remember once buying into a video-recording system when I changed the way we did lesson observations to offer more self-reflection. It was an expensive investment that fell flat because we quickly realised that staff actually found lesson reviews, conversations and reflections more useful than watching themselves on video afterwards.

Stage 3: Mirror mirror

Review and reflection on lessons learnt

When thinking about the stages of change it is important to consider the review schedule. Usually I see it at critical points in the three stages and try to think of the focus for the review.

I will review Stage 1, the *why and what*, for clarity. Are we clear on what we are going to do?

At Stage 2 there will be a range of approaches to the review. We need to think and reflect on the implementation of the change and be able to respond to it. By linking it back to Stage 1 we can keep asking: Are we doing what we said we would do? If not, why not? There may be good reason to change as we develop. Is that by design or accident, or are we ignoring the reasons why the change process is going to fail?

We also need to understand that in the short term there is likely to be a false result – either it is going absolutely smoothly and seems to be working perfectly (the honeymoon period) or it is a complete disaster and everyone is opposed to it and has clear reasons as to why it is not working. In both cases, we need to be careful not to overreact. I tend to find that when I knee-jerk react to situations which are not going to plan there is a real danger that we lose that original clarity and purpose and create something that is far from our original intention and risks not addressing the original problem. Therefore, when reviewing Stage 2 I invite a lot of narrative, on-the-ground comments and conversations. Often, in reviewing, we go to data and facts and there is an important place for them, but in the implementation stage I also feel that what we see and hear also matters a lot, especially to the staff who are on the front line of the change process.

This is the end ...

I love to cycle and have made it my go-to exercise over the last few years (since my knees told me to stop running). When I go out on longer, more strenuous rides I set out parameters about what it will take for me to stop or quit. It could be the weather, how my fitness levels feel, a crash, puncture or getting lost. What I am effectively saying to myself is 'If I lose my vision, physical ability or motivation, I will stop. This may be forced or otherwise'. That does not mean everything will get better though; stopping 40 miles into a ride still means you need to get home. What helps me is knowing that if the worst happens and I feel like I cannot continue, I can make this better through stopping. Quitting is not the end because I will ride another day – I can start again. The truth of the matter is that, apart from one or two falls off my bike, I have only ever quit when I have been unable to overcome the mental blocks I faced during the ride. Even cut, bruised and bloodied I have got back on my bike, but when I have lost the desire, vision or will, I find continuing almost impossible – that's the point at which I have phoned to get a lift home. When implementing change it is rarely physical barriers such as money or resources that have stopped me. Like riding, I find the mental blocks, my own and other people's, the hardest obstacles to overcome. Knowing this means that I think extra hard about what those mental blocks might be when planning change.

I think about myself within the change process in the same way I think about planning a longer ride. When do I say I am happy and the process has ended? The distance travelled is enough and we can stop and focus on another project. What happens if we say we have gone far enough and we are happy to stop? Knowing the distance you need to travel to get the job done is important. Sometimes – especially if that distance is not really known – we face uncertainty, and that is when the mental blocks are usually their strongest.

Don't be a complete (insert your own expletive)

When does change become embedded and how do we know?

As I have said, the change process needs to be followed up on, reviewed, analysed and evaluated. We need to be brave enough to drop it if it is not successful, but give it enough time to be effective. A big mistake is 'knee-jerk leadership' where leaders switch from one idea to the next, fuelled by the zeitgeist of popular approaches as seen on Twitter, or in the media and sometimes based on what others tell us Ofsted wants.

Ultimately, when we set out on that change process in our school the original intentions which we outlined at the beginning of the process need to stand the test of time. If, at the end, we can go back to our original purpose and see that we have kept true to it then we know we have been successful. It is like a game of Chinese Whispers where everyone involved kept to the plan because it was simple and clear, and as it comes back to us we can nod and think – yes, that is why we did this.

On reflection, we need to know that we made this change happen without destroying other people along the way and kept our integrity. So often, I have seen people thrust change through and not really care what others think or feel. They have pushed, bullied or lectured the change across a staffroom that was often too scared to speak out. I have found that we can make change happen without being – in my own words – a 'dick' about it (please use the expletive you are most comfortable with). By not being a 'dick', I can reflect back and feel that the change happened because it was the best thing – not driven by fear of the leader. I still believe that other people's dignity matters, as much as mine does. If the change works, do not go around telling everyone 'I told you so', and likewise if it does not work, do not blame all those who blocked it along the way.

Conclusion

Managing and leading change is never easy, but if we apply a few guidelines to the process we can ensure that we go into the procedure with a better chance of making it a success:

- Knowing why we are making the change – what impact it will have that is better than what we already have
- Communicating the need for change and the process for its implementation to others as clearly as possible
- Understanding how to manage people within this process; their drivers, fears and needs – supporting them through the process
- Knowing what the outcome is going to be and planning how to get there – understanding the short-term and long-term goals
- Never being afraid to stop, change direction or say this is good enough. As long as this is communicated along the process and we are clear why we make these decisions then I have never worried about having to force a change through that has either failed to have the intended impact, lost momentum or is no longer needed. It's a brave thing to do but far more effective than pushing forward with something everyone knows is doomed to fail. It's about understanding that this is also part of the change process itself – that every project will not always be a success but the process itself will help us better understand what we are trying to achieve
- Oh … and don't be a complete @~£%

7

On Finance and Business

In this chapter we will explore the importance of understanding how finance and business work in a school setting. We will cover the following topics:

- Budget setting, monitoring and control
- Long-term and short-term strategic planning
- Risk management
- Why understanding the school as a business is just as important as understanding the impact of teaching and learning on pupils

Introduction

When I was 17 I opened a record shop; it lasted almost two years. I was passionate about music but I had no idea how to run an effective business. The same is true of school leadership: understanding how teachers teach and children learn is not enough if you want to be a good school leader and run an effective school. Though much of this has changed recently due to multi-academy trusts where finance and organisational pressures are taken away from the day-to-day responsibilities of many school leaders, I still strongly believe that having a good understanding of your school's financial backbone is vital in making the what, how and why of our educational vision a reality.

I have heard it said that it is logistics and not strategy that leaders need to understand before they develop a vision for the future. This is true of school leadership. You can have the greatest plans and the vision of all visions and know exactly what needs to be done to improve your school but, if you cannot understand, organise, utilise, finance and maintain the resources needed to achieve your ambitions then your ideas will become words and dreams unfulfilled. A good school leader needs to know how to manage a lot of 'stuff' that seems to have little to do with children learning how to read and write. Therefore, school leaders need to develop a skill set very much removed from their days as a classroom teacher and become far more corporate in their approach to education. For many this is something that does not come naturally and feels removed from the reason they became a teacher.

The leader of stuff

When I have asked new school leaders, or those applying for the role, what they are most worried about when taking on a head teacher role it is the unknown aspects of finance and the running of the school business that are usually the main reasons given. There's good reason for this. In almost every position before the top job in a school there is little real accountability for running the business of the school and its future financial sustainability, success or failure. In fact, it would seem that more and more, through the development of academy trusts, even head teachers might have a limited role in budget setting, human resources or site management. What is important is that even without full control over these areas of school management, a good understanding of the possibilities and barriers available go a long way in helping us to develop a vision and secure consistent and effective provision. You may not control the purse strings but you need to sell the vision for improvement and therefore you need to know how this will be viable and cost effective at a time when money is very tight in our schools.

You can go right through the leadership hierarchy as a senior leader and deputy head teacher and never have full responsibility for more than a small budget or be on the periphery of decisions about budgets or structural organisation. This is also true about the general day-to-day running of a school business where there is a whole new world of things to know about that can derail your true purpose and have nothing to do with teaching and learning. As mentioned in Chapter 1, 'On Leadershit', these distractions not only can have a huge impact on the direction and success of your leadership but they also present real threats to the wellbeing of the school leader. Some of the business aspects can present as leadershit, but their impact can be far more damaging if ignored or misunderstood.

In my time as a head teacher I have had to deal with many issues: the maintenance and development of the site grounds and school building and many complications which have had a huge impact on teaching and learning, limiting space and being very expensive as well as taking up a huge amount of my time. Collapsed drains, leaky roofs and potholes all had a major impact on the smooth running of my schools. Unless you take over a new build, and experience tells me these are never simple and often bring problems of their own, most school buildings and sites are a little like fragile and ill-tempered elderly relatives needing constant attention and love – this is often expensive, is very time consuming, and involves you developing a different mindset and skill set from those you had in your teaching and early leadership days. Keeping on top of this aspect of school leadership often directs your attention towards the (and this is a personal view) very dull world of logistics, maintenance and regulations.

Using collapsed drains as one example, we found out six months before work began that this problem was serious; collapsed drains were not on the School Development Plan that year. The smell was random and at times quite unbearable. On occasions we would have a foul flooding across one side of the school site that disrupted playtimes and shut down parts of the school building. We began to dread the rain. The constant stream of very expensive plumbers cost us incredible amounts but also disrupted the daily running of the provision. When the true extent of the problem was discovered the cost to solve it was more than £100,000. We spent time and money writing a funding bid which was unsuccessful because of one small point (they said there was not enough evidence that we had done remedial work); we then spent more months contesting this decision (showing them over 80 invoices that illustrated the remedial work) but also went ahead with the work, which took seven weeks, shut down the staff car park and caused all sorts of local and logistical planning issues around site access and safety. On top of all this, the money came from the school budget and this meant there was a knock-on impact on other projects and resources we had planned as part of our school development cycle.

Operational issues can also have a big impact on the way your school is run: alarms going off in the middle of the night waking your community at 4am; rabbits with myxomatosis slowly dying on the school field; a badger set found underneath a Portakabin. The fact is you cannot ignore any of these events. You have to manage them and they always seem to happen at the most inconvenient times, such as in the middle of an Ofsted inspection or during a critical part of the moderation cycle where your time is precious and every moment in your diary is booked up. In 2022 I got the Ofsted call during staff shortages due to the Covid-19 pandemic; I had planned to cover a class the next day because we could not get a supply teacher and had no one else available. It would not have been in the best interests of the Academy if I was in class during an Ofsted inspection, so we had to find a way to cover the class. You have to be able to adapt your plans at short notice and sometimes finding a Plan B needs you to dig deep and think creatively. An important aspect in all of this is how you learn to balance conflicting priorities, but also, if necessary, pivoting and changing the direction of your focus fully at the right time. There is no point covering a lesson when an Ofsted inspector is wading through a stream of effluent running down the Key Stage 1 corridor (though it would probably be worth a photograph), but equally teaching children is our primary duty.

Working 9 to 5 - ha!

Your school may also be used for additional services and extended school provisions, holiday clubs, after-school clubs, local community clubs and organisations such as tai chi, church services or the neighbourhood watch. Just recently we hired out our school site for a wedding of an ex-pupil. There is something exciting about placing your school at the heart of the community; it is also a way of finding additional revenue when money is tight. Though these things are very rarely under your direct leadership, the school leader needs to understand this bigger picture when future planning your provision, utilising budgets or handling public and school relations. From complaints about amenities not working properly to rooms being double booked you need to have this sense of your whole school as an entity beyond 9am to 5pm from September to July, and the impact this has on what kind of an organisation you are or want to be.

At my current school we only close for one week of the year (Christmas Eve to New Year's Day). During the summer, we have well more than 100 children aged between 0 and 18 on site from 7:30am to 6pm. This includes children with very complex special educational needs as well as emergency social care placements. I am lucky to have an amazing business manager with the experience and skill set to run this provision across the summer, but I am still the designated safeguarding lead, I am still the person with ultimate responsibility and account-ability. I cannot just walk away on the last day of the summer term, singing Alice Cooper's 'Schools Out' as I skip away clicking my heels. This is one of the biggest changes anyone finds in the step up to headship. The feelings of responsibility and accountability vary but they never leave you. As a teacher the summer hol-idays feel like a total release because you almost always hand over your class and await a new one in September. That never happens as the head teacher. You don't rewind and start over again. Your time as school leader never pauses or stops. This doesn't mean you cannot go away and unwind, but it is the biggest change most school leaders notice when they step into the head teacher role – that they are always feeling responsible and accountable. The children may not be at school during the holidays, but the chance that someone might break into the building and steal your laptops certainly increases.

I have learnt to find ways to have my summer break but also understand what is happening at my school, and therefore I am mindful that for many at my school the year is not September to July. While most staff are getting ready for their summer holidays I also have many staff who work all year round. This small adjustment in how I approach the end of the academic year was an important change because there's nothing worse than a head teacher who does not understand the context of their school and cannot represent everyone within it. If I went around in the last week of the summer term as though we were all about to have a big holiday I would find that I had lost the respect of about a quarter of my staff. This important adjustment to my leadership took me years to get right, but it is vital to understand that in the very likely event that before you became the leader of a school your experiences were as a class teacher or senior leader not as a teaching assistant, cleaner or business man-ager. The leader needs to understand the school through the eyes of everyone. Step back and see that they are not all class-based staff. Education is about much more than children in lessons learning and teachers teaching, it is about organisations and how effectively they are run. It is about the kitchen staff, office staff, contractors and cleaners. Often, I hear people say that the business side of running a school is not as important as the teaching side. I cannot emphasise this strongly enough: if you want to be a good leader in education and you want good teaching and learning, make sure that you are also sharp-ening your understanding of the business side of school as well.

The business of school – do things better

The truth is, unless you came from a different profession, there is very little preparation you can gain for the many areas that can arise once you take to the seat of the school leader. Even if you are given opportunities as you develop to take on budgets and be in finance and strategic budget planning meetings, the reality is these decisions feel different when you are the school leader and fully accountable for them. Therefore, early in any headship it is very likely you will sit down with either a finance assistant, business manager or grounds manager or take a call from a human resource manager, and what they say will have a massive impact on what you will need to do in the following days, weeks or months. You may have a vision for teaching and learning, but leading a school is about having a vision for the whole community, including the very fabric of the building. Understanding the many intricate and complex patterns that exist and play out within that community, beyond knowing whether your children are learning, is vital in the longevity and ambitions you will have for your time as a school leader. At its heart a good school leader needs to understand the logistics behind their organisation.

The resources available to us and our capacity to deliver them effectively drive our ability to fulfil any improvement plans we have for our school. We need to understand this as early as possible in our leadership post and it then becomes a constant cycle of review to make sure we are always on top of this business side – even though, for many of us, it is something we don't enjoy as much as the other sides of the role. This is why staff who do know this stuff really well need to be given time with you on a regular basis to ensure that there are no surprises around the corner. I have always prioritised my diary to meet with my business manager because they often line-manage finance, human resources and the grounds. They have such a vital role to play in making your life as a leader of learning far more manageable, but you have to understand that they usually have a very different perspective on the life of the school.

When supporting school leaders I have met with many who have struggled leading the business of school. I have seen them lament their great plans failing, or just not having the impact they wanted, and in almost every case you can chart the failures back to the business plan. Ideas on paper often work in principle (they always work in my head), but it is always the reality that makes the difference, and often in education this is the area that is given the least time and strategy. We can't create virtual reality simulators to play our expensive plans out in a safe environment. We have to understand why we are making the plans, the costs, the implementation challenges and the expected impact in the planning stage because once we start there will be financial commitments that can be extremely far-reaching if unsuccessful. For example, implementing a reading strategy that will have far-reaching benefits with well-chosen research, evidence of success in a similar context, good materials and resources, will almost always fail if you can't get the people, funding and structures in place to deliver it. I often find that 90% of the time and effort in a strategy is spent on the *what* rather than the *how*. However, it is the boring logistics that make the plan work: careful funding that will see the project through, good recruitment, a collective understanding on how the implementation will work within the current structures, understanding what impact looks like, line-management structures, trainings and inductions. All of these other aspects are rarely planned at the beginning and are an afterthought. They should be central to the plan when the idea is first given the green light.

People and time are the most important resources a school has, but how they fit into the other aspects of the business plan will be the difference between building a successful school or not. The importance of finance and the effective running of the operational aspects cannot be underestimated. My insistence on running a good business is critical to ensuring children get the best education we can provide. That means we plan to 'do things better'. I am not interested in being world class, the best or inspirational or other such rubbish often associated with the business world. I want us to 'do things better'. If that means my business manager invests 30 hours of their time so that solar panels can be installed to save £3,000 a year, I think about the longer-term benefits – or lack of them. Will this make things better for us? For a reception cohort, seven years of this saving amounts to £21,000 by the time they leave in Year 6. As I write this, energy prices are rising at an increasing rate but the panels have been in place for six years and are still going strong, and we can see how they have helped us offset some of the pain that the additional energy costs have brought in. When I leave, they will still be saving the school money, and they will also be sending a strong environmental message to the community. Money is not the only 'better' I thought about. As a school, saving hundreds of tons on our carbon emissions is another organisational decision that I took into consideration, setting a sustainable action that generations of children and our community could see is just as important as the money in this decision.

Planning for long-term legacy needs to put the sustainable financial implications first, but other considerations will play out when we think: Are we making things better? We cannot forget that budgets in schools are tight and becoming ever more challenging. If you cannot afford to run the school, it will impact on that most important of resources – people, and therefore the quality of your provision.

Budget setting – money's too tight to mention

The head teacher standards are clear that school leaders need to:

> Prioritise and allocate financial resources appropriately, ensuring efficiency, effectiveness and probity in the use of public funds. (Department for Education, 2020)

I often dream what I would do if I won the EuroMillions. I have decided I want a top floor penthouse flat in the Barbican Centre. I saw one for £5.5 million pounds in 2022. In the real world the fact is I have never bought a EuroMillions ticket and therefore this will never happen. Money is only an effective tool if you have it. We need this mindset when working with our budgets within our schools. We need to ground ourselves in the reality of how our budget works and base everything upon this reality with a ruthless efficiency.

Budget setting is a critical point in the school calendar year. The time of year will vary depending on what type of school you are in, but the implications for the coming 12 months are about as important as it gets in education. Get the budget wrong and the fallout can be extremely damaging and far-reaching. This can have a short-term impact, but more importantly, if we are not careful, we can end up positioning the organisation into a long-term crisis that will eventually require drastic action to rectify. Therefore, budget setting can be full of tension, ambiguity and difficult and conflicting decisions about which priorities you need to focus on. There are many issues you will need to consider, which we will now outline.

Managing a deficit budget which resulted in having to make cuts and redundancies was, without doubt, one of the most challenging I have had as a head teacher, and needed some of the hardest decision making. The tension between making or not making a position redundant is a constant bedfellow when I am budgeting, especially in areas where the amounts are in the tens of thousands. I always focus on the position and not the people when thinking about whether a redundancy needs to be made – though in the reality of the process it is almost impossible not to think about people because it is such an emotive process, and unless you have no heart it will weigh heavily upon you throughout.

Making people redundant is one of the hardest things a school leader has to do. The process is brutal. You have to think carefully about what you need to do but this is different from what you want to do, and often in a redundancy situation what you choose to 'not' do. Systemic change in which roles are made redundant is a horrible situation to find yourself in and I have seen, too often, leaders try to do everything possible to avoid the redundancy and in the process make a situation that was inevitable much worse.

The cuts you can make in most areas of school are often small. Cutting the photocopying budget by 5% will not make a massive difference, but this process is cumulative and therefore cutting on some resources, curriculum equipment, photocopying, tea, coffee and visitor 'refreshments' can add up to the thousands. They also have a very negative whole-school impact, especially in the short term. When you need to find savings in the thousands you may be able to find this in funding streams away from staffing, but for bigger amounts you will have to look at your staffing budget because most schools aim to spend between 70 and 80% of their budget on staffing.

The first rule of understanding your financial position in a school is about the cost of staffing and how sustainable this is. For some schools, already in a deficient position, your staffing has to balance year after year. When making changes, going over by a few thousand can end up making redundancy inevitable within years. Therefore, staff structure and future planning are vital within the budget-setting cycle and the areas I spend the most time on. If you ever look down into the expenditure of a school's budget you will often see areas overspent. I remember the first time I saw a budget that was 1,000% overspent and having a minor heart attack. Then I looked at the amount and saw the original budget was only £20. OK, not an ideal situation but it was not going to break the bank – whereas a 4% overspend on your staffing budget will have a massive impact:

1,000% of £20 is £200

4% of £1,600,000 is £64,000

Since I have been a head teacher my rule of thumb has been that staffing expenditure is roughly between 70 and 80% of our budget. It is vital that this one budget stream is your most closely guarded and planned area within any budget-setting process and that any recruitment is very carefully considered in the context of this.

With staffing you can initially advertise for a fixed-term position which allows you the luxury of the post ending within a year and buys time to assess the sustainability of the post. The problem with this is you want brilliant staff and you limit your pool of candidates when there is no stability in the post offered. This is another important area to consider and another area that often causes problems.

Know the difference between a one-off investment and a long-term investment

This is often the biggest mistake I see in early leadership where finance is an issue. The leader's vision was so driven that they took the early plunge to ensure they could see it out and in the process they ended up struggling financially. In times of plenty, or a surplus budget, we are better placed to make long-term commitments and investments. Even then we need to be careful – one additional member of staff over time can easily add in an extra £30,000 a year and over £100,000 to the budget over four years. Spending £30,000 on a one-off project is much easier to plan and account for than sustaining this investment over time.

The dangerous myth of more

One of the most dangerous myths I have constantly come across in schools is 'more is better'. In particular, this is often centred upon people or money. There is this idea that if people leave then life will become unbearable in the school, but no one individual is, or should be, thought of as irreplaceable. There is also the argument that more money will solve the problem. Schools need to be funded better, but they are not, and therefore wishing for a money tree is just a waste of time. We need to make the best of what we have got, even when we make our case for more funding and the counter-argument that less money and continued efficiencies improve performance. That more is always better and less is a disaster is not the full story. The truth is that throwing money at a problem is often a recipe for disaster, and rarely sustainable. Schools, along with children, are able to morph and adapt to any changes that happen. It just needs careful future planning. A head teacher might be in a school for 20 years and the community may love them and see them as an effective and brilliant leader. The reality is that when they leave they will be forgotten in terms of day-to-day functionality within a few terms at most (in reality, within a week). The role will need to be filled with a new head teacher, but not all roles need to keep on going as they did. Even school leader roles have changed over the years. The same can be said of teachers, learning mentors, office staff, care-takers, governors, sports coaches or teaching assistants. I have never heard of a school finding £30,000 stuck down the back of an interactive whiteboard, therefore we have to treat finances very carefully at all times. We usually know our budgets pretty far in advance – give or take a small increase or decrease; therefore, we need to budget within our resources and always think ahead and build our plans around this reality.

Early on in one of my headships I had to make more than £250,000 of cuts in the budget. This huge amount meant I had to plan a restructure and make a considerable number of redundancies. Once I had finished the business plan I shared it with all the stakeholders, including parents. I was new to the school community and wanted to impress them, but here I was cutting the budget and my 'so-called' leadership was now seen as 'taking away from the school', making it weaker. I still remember the parent session with a sense of dread, a busy school hall and many angry and emotional people. At one point a parent whose child was very unwell stood up and said to me, 'On your head be it!'. She was crying as she said it. What do you say to that? I felt terrible, but it changed nothing. I still made those people redundant. If I hadn't, the school would have been hundreds of thousands of pounds in debt within a few years. Many years later we were functioning at least as well and no longer had a deficit budget. That parent was also singing the praises of the school and the provision for their child. Weathering moments and sticking to difficult decisions is critical, even when every fibre of your soul is screaming at you to stop what you are doing.

Living in the moment in schools is something that can be a great challenge. In the moment all can seem lost. I remember the business meeting in which the cuts were agreed and the dates set for telling the staff. I had not been at the school for long and I felt terrible that my early legacy was one of taking away, breaking down what was seen from the outside as a brilliant school and making it less. In that moment I couldn't see the future and therefore I just felt the awful sense of a journey that I didn't want to take and didn't really know where I would end up. I could have asked the governors to take on the process but knew that I had to do it – it was vitally important in terms of my role as school leader that I did it and looked each and every person in the eye as I did. I believe that learning to get through these moments is another key reason I have been a head teacher for so long. In every situation where, in the moment, I have felt powerless and wanted to run away there is always a future moment where, on reflection, I have felt proud that I managed my way through it and almost always look back to realise that the decision was the right one and for the better. There is nothing wrong with imposter syndrome when the decisions are so critical. Even though in every case I still feel that I cannot take it for granted that it will be alright in the end, and there is still that niggling sense that this is awful and I want it to disappear, I still steady myself for making the right long-term decision despite this uneasy feeling.

False profits

Clairvoyance – which is from the French *clair*, meaning 'clear' and *voyance* meaning 'vision' – is something every school leader wants to have. It would be a great gift in dealing with the future challenges a school faces but it does not take a genius to work out that clairvoyance can be explained as the result of hallucinations, self-delusion, overworking, not enough coffee, and confirmation or expectancy bias – basically, a failure to appreciate probabilities grounded in the facts rather than a reliance on paranormal behaviour. This is why setting a budget beyond one year is one of my pet hates. It just cannot be done accurately. I have tried to set them for almost two decades and they have always become a mess a few weeks after setting them. For example, you might have made £10,000 profit from lettings this year, but can you factor that in next year? What if the Tai Chi club moves to the new sports centre that is being built in town? You may have it on good intelligence that things will stay the same, you may even have someone's *word* that they will stick with you; the stark reality is that situations change constantly and setting a budget on the status quo is often a very risky way to do it. You cannot take your previous budget for granted, ever.

The intelligence you have is often flawed because you cannot predict the future beyond the basic funding of numbers and predicted percentage rises or caps. Even then, that is not enough for a two-year budget, never mind a three- or five-year one. What happens when you try to predict future budgets is it almost always looks terrible and this in turn creates barriers when you want to plan; it makes you scared. It is of course prudent to future plan your budget, but I no longer allow it to dictate my ambitions. Again, the important thing to remember is it is not the cost of toilet rolls, pencils or the little extras that usually take you into a deficit budget – it is the bigger longer-term commitments around staffing that you always have to keep the closest eye on. When you think about staffing you can predict the future structure more accurately and therefore make more stable longer-term budget decisions.

The next GREAT thing

Another issue within budget setting is the fact that everyone wants to sell you the *new best thing*. Consultants tell you that they want to make your life easier and tech companies have the answer to all your woes, for a price. It is easy to buy into all this 'new stuff' and feel that you are doing what is right for the school. Experience has taught me, time and time again, that on most occasions new whizzy systems for lesson observations, expensive software for school improvement or integrated report writing tools often mask a very simple challenge within effective school leadership. That leaders need to have first-hand, face-to-face experience with the problems and the challenges they need to overcome before they make substantial monetary and staff investment. I can pay thousands of pounds to a consultant to help me understand my school better, but deep down that masks the greatest problem – that someone who should know more than the consultant doesn't. What I find when going in to support schools is that the leadership usually knows exactly what the problem is, they just lack the confidence, capacity or knowledge about how to solve it. We often do it for validation, and in most cases the consultant tells you what you already knew, and in many cases have no better ideas (and certainly no accountability) to make it better. The same can apply to software and innovations. They advertise as being the answer to problems that need deeper understanding and investigation rather than the quick fix.

I am not saying that all systems and consultants are worthless; far from it. But when planning for what can often be a big financial commitment think very carefully why you need them and consider the following:

- Your knowledge and understanding of the problem you want to address
- Your ability to solve the problem without creating more work, or challenge for your staff

- What you could do before you make any major commitments – it's only when you can't see any other way forward that I believe you should think more seriously about changing systems or buying in additional help
- Are you trying to buy your way out of making an unpopular or difficult decision or using the consultant as the scapegoat for them?

The challenges of different provisions

There are other factors that are usually contextual but worth exploring a little that can make a big difference to your finances and business plans. Running a nursery provision on site presents real difficulties in planning a budget. It is difficult to predict what hours parents may want from week to week. As families have used nurseries more and at an earlier age we have found that we have had to change our business plan completely. Our mainstream nursery is open all year round from 7.30am to 6pm to meet the needs of our community. As mentioned, staffing is your most important and expensive resource, and with nursery provision you have to meet certain ratios at certain ages and therefore need a core staff. Another issue is people want security and continuity in their job. We have found that the use of our nursery fluctuates throughout the year and it is very difficult to balance nursery budgets and inconsistent staffing. Therefore, we look at the benefits of our nursery in terms of the long-term impact it has on building relationships, supporting children and families and developing our own expertise as an organisation. Sometimes in leadership, you need to understand that the positives are not always financial but you can never lose sight of what the financial impact is.

The same can be said of my current school's specialist provision. We currently run a 50-place special school within our mainstream setting. Funding for specialist provision is different from mainstream SEND funding. We get a set amount per place plus top-up funding between £5,000 and £25,000 depending on the need identified in the child's Education and Health Care Plan. Funding a specialist provision on this scale within a mainstream school brings financial and professional benefits. We have one senior team including the head teacher; the same building is used so fuel economies can be made; professional services can be shared; training can be conducted across the site and utilities and resources can be shared. There are also the incredible benefits from shared knowledge and understanding as well as the many benefits that come about when children with a huge range of needs and talents are all learning in the same place. There are also a number of incredibly challenging factors though. When one child with complex needs leaves there is a huge budget implication that can range from £15,000 to £35,000 coming out of the budget. Each year I have 8–15 children in specialist provision in Year 6 and leaving us at the end of the academic year; we rarely know which new children are joining us until late in the summer term. That can amount to hundreds of thousands of pounds in lost income, and once again, the biggest cost and most important resource in this provision is the staff. To run a specialist provision you need a stable staff at all times.

Staffing, staffing, staffing

As I have said many times, getting your staffing right is critical. Too few staff and you can have wellbeing and capacity problems that can have a school-wide impact. Overstaff and you can find yourself having to go through future redundancy procedures. Both of these scenarios are hard lessons for any school leader. I spend the most time during budget setting working on the staffing element of the plan:

1. I talk to leaders looking at best- and worst-case staffing for the coming year. There is little flex with class teachers but more with additional supporting staff. Again, you have to think about ratios with younger children
2. I have an open document that I then share with senior leaders (as early as January) and in this I set out my thoughts for staffing, where people will be (year group, class and cover, etc.) in the following September. I always include my business manager in this so that we know where *everyone* will be. We also plan which rooms will be used
3. In the back of my mind is sustainability. It never leaves me. I often advertise a newly planned post as fixed term because unless I am 100% sure about a new post I need to see it in action to know whether it will be viable and effective

Another critical area to spend time on when thinking about staffing is contingency planning. Staff will leave for promotions, get pregnant, change career, get better offers, relocate, become disillusioned with education (or your school) and many other reasons, which means you will be left with a space to cover, usually with little time to think about it. My first thought in these situations is always – *do we need to do what we have always been doing?* Sometimes, this is an easy answer – yes, we need a Year 6 teacher. On other occasions, I see it as an opportunity. Once you commit to staffing you pledge to either a set time cost or a long-term ongoing cost. Therefore, I often do not replace positions outside of class teachers immediately, especially if their impact is difficult to find good evidence for. In smaller schools you may not have this flexibility, but if you do it is a good way to take an opportunity to review your provision and develop its remit.

In the past I have not automatically replaced positions such as learning mentors; instead we have advertised for an 'emotional literacy support assistant' and set the system up so they worked more within the classroom and alongside the teacher, rather than having children being taken out to work in isolation. It is lovely when you have a stable staffing situation; I also look at the change that comes through staff leaving as an opportunity to improve what we do. Sometimes this is because of financial necessity, but if you make it standard practice, it becomes a strategic tool for developing your most important resource – your staff.

Strategic sanctuary

You need to spend time thinking about your systems and how they ensure that you are making long-term growth sustainable. This takes time. Even with experience in this area, when you join a new school you need to understand it before you make too many radical changes. I have often tinkered with systems thinking I have improved them only to go back to the original system a few years later. This is why making time in your schedule to be able to move away from firefighting or dealing with the leadershit is vital. Having a place where you can think strategically about the business of education allows you to invest in the future. I have heard this space called 'strategic sanctuary'. It can be a place or a time. The important thing is acknowledging that this is what you are doing, that you are in a place where you can think about things critically and openly. If you can create this with others within your organisation, it can become even more powerful. I have seen people organise away days, or meetings in coffee shops, but for me it is as simple as creating a safe place in work where ideas, review and reflection are open and honest.

Conclusion: Good business sense

Good school leaders are good business leaders. They understand the impact that financial planning, management and control can have on the quality of education their school provides. They leverage their business skills to get the best outcomes, generate funding, plan targeted and risk-aware projects and never lose sight of their overall aim – which is as simple as:

• Setting a balanced budget within means that is carefully monitored at regular points in the year

- Always knowing what the long-term plan is and how the short-term elements of the budget are leading to this outcome – keep asking, why are we doing this?
- Knowing what the risks are. Make sure your governors know what those risks are – have a risk register that is shared. A risk register is a simple RAG - (red, amber, green) rated list of potential risks to the school organisation. They need to be contextual and they are a good discussion/ activity to do with school governors. In the past I have had a risk register that has had the following on it: head teacher leaving, dropping numbers coming to the school, significantly low SATs results, new school being built in the town and struggles to recruit staff
- If you have a business manager, making sure they are a central part of your senior team. They can be the most important resource a school has. If you do not, then try to think outside of the teaching and learning box and ask – what would a commercial business do in this situation?

As I have said, there's nothing wrong in thinking like a business when thinking like a school leader. You are not out to make millions but you are out to make children's lives better and successful – I cannot think of a better business plan.

Reference

Department for Education (2020) Headteachers' standards 2020. Available at: www.gov.uk/government/publications/national-standards-of-excellence-for-headteachers [accessed 28.10.22].

8
On Rebellious Leadership

This final chapter will explore how school leaders need a rebellious streak. It will cover the following areas:

- Leaders need to learn to lead, not follow others, even when they give good and sage advice – leadership is about confidence and experience. It is about the lessons learnt, often the hard way
- Be political but not party political
- You cannot run a school on love alone
- Tame your ego – but still do it your way

Introduction

In this concluding chapter, I want to bring together some of the key principles that have helped me through the years I have had in education, and continue to look forward to having, as a head teacher. I say *want* because as I began to write I realised that much of this book is not about definite rules and regulations for successful school leadership – in fact this is a paradox. Maybe I should have said this earlier.

There is no blueprint for successful school leadership, no map or set of rules or exact guidance to get you through. Leading a school starts when you enter the maze, by which time you have already passed the point of no return and you just have to find a way through it. Yes, we can listen to others and take their advice, but ultimately it is all about you. If there is a theme running throughout this book, it is self-confidence: knowing yourself within the leadership role as you make your journey through it. It goes back to your core purpose.

Throughout my career as a school leader, I have always wanted to feel that I have done what is right for my schools and communities. There is also a very strong element of doing what is 'safe', balancing the risks we take because making too many mistakes damages our confidence to keep going. Leadership is often lonely and scary. No one can fully prepare you for this and it only truly becomes apparent once you sit in the head teacher's chair. At times the risks we take to ensure that we lead an effective school can feel almost overwhelming, especially when we are navigating through the unknown. As I have mentioned before, your longevity and personal fulfilment in the role are the only real tests of success in education. Longevity in leadership is just as much about the difficulties of climbing the peaks, as planting flags at the summit and the hair-raising descents. Those who have weathered the hardest times know that there are moments when they feel totally lost at sea but they also know, through experience, that there is opportunity to grow stronger and wiser within the crisis. The looming abyss of failure is also full of opportunity. What often stops us is a lack of appetite for the risk. The 'feel the fear and do it anyway' approach is easy to talk about but very hard to implement when you are under huge pressure and feeling the accountability weighing heavy. Therefore, we need to explore some important questions:

- How do we find meaning, even in the most challenging of contexts?
- How do we harness our personal strengths in leading our schools?
- How do we know ourselves and become confident enough to follow our instincts?

So let us start with a list:

- Avoid the leadershit through focusing on what *really* matters
- Don't pretend this is not a business

- Learn to breathe; know yourself in crisis
- Let your teachers teach
- Never take inclusion for granted
- Do not follow the crowd; listen to your staff, especially when trying to make changes
- Learn to stand up when you want to hide
- Build teams that make you feel challenged and supported, that can make decisions that matter
- There is no end game, just evolution; you'll never find that pot of gold at the end of the rainbow

This is quite an interesting task to do. What would your one-liner words of advice have been to yourself when you started out in education? What would you say to others if they took over your role tomorrow? Write the list.

Rebel rebel

I have come to understand that there is a thread of rebellion running through me. An energy and resistance to standing still or feeling that I have reached a destination. Two words have followed me since I was a teenager and they seemed to be part of my leadership strategy in headship: punk and rebellion. I have done much reflecting on this and come to understand that I am proud of these two words within my approaches towards leadership, not because they make me feel less bored by the humdrum daily routines but because I feel they add a weight of importance and purpose to the role I have as school leader. They have an attitude and conviction about them that support a 'do-it-yourself' sense of innovation while still feeling like I am part of the education tribe, of something bigger – even when it is confrontational. They are words that conjure a strong history of energy and creativity. More than this, I see them at the heart of my moral purpose.

Changing the world – one lesson at a time

I am regularly asked, 'Why did you want to be a head?'. Sometimes followed by, 'Are you mad?'. The answer is simple. I want to make a real difference and I believe that I cannot do that without doing what I believe is right. I need to be confident enough to challenge the status quo, especially when it is ineffective, because if I do not then what purpose do I have?

Now I know that the definition of punk can mean a 'worthless person' and for some its anti-establishment undertones seem at odds with a school leader.

I do not see it this way though. I see rebellion and a punk attitude as a positive way of leading in a school. I am not thinking about ripped bondage clothes, safety pins through noses and multi-coloured Mohican hairstyles, smashing the system or complete anarchy. I am thinking about the inventiveness, bravery and desire to not do things just because that is how we are expected to do them, or always have done them. I believe that rebellion is a vital part of what the school leader needs to understand when leading within a school. It is about developing a leader, not follower, mindset and standing up for what we believe is the right thing to do within the context we are in.

We really do not need a generation of school leaders who look to others to justify the decisions they need to make in their school. So many critical decisions are made or created through national policy, governmental initiatives and Ofsted and much of the time they do not translate well at a local level. They do not always meet the needs of village schools, or inner-city schools, because they are far too universal. A one-size-fits-all method cannot work when no two schools or communities are ever exactly the same. Therefore, the leader needs to be confident enough to 'flick the V' and say – 'This is how we do it here', or even 'We are not doing that'. For rebellion to exist though, the school leader must feel that they are justified in their actions, and I believe that we develop this as teachers and then need to continue to develop it as leaders. It is a narrative we should be proud of, but also careful with. I can look back into my early headship and see what seems like an angrier and often braver head teacher than I see today, boycotting SATs and marching with unions. Today, I am more defiant in many ways and yet my rebellion is quieter and less public.

Anger is an energy – the political school leader

I was in northern France a few years ago when the farmers were revolting. They knew how to protest, dumping tons of manure at the entrances and exits to the motorways and onto the roundabouts – then lighting it up. They upset everyone. They just seemed not to care because they were passionately opposed to what was happening regarding their now and their future. I do not see this angry rebellious spirit in education; if I do, it just comes across as moaning. I only pay my expensive union subscription because I 'might' need their legal support; otherwise, I have no idea what they do to really stand up on the issues affecting me as a school leader. This is probably unfair, but it is their job to convince me they are and currently they do not. Therefore, I see the community of head teachers as the real power in influencing the political landscape, but we have never been more divided. The fragmented education system has pulled us apart. There are pockets of voice but ultimately most head teachers I know are busy getting on with running their schools or trying to get time with their families. We do not have that angry farmer energy. Now, I am not suggesting that we all pile marking on the M25, but if you are unhappy with the direction of education I really believe that you should let this be known, loud and clear.

I have heard it said that I am too political and I should focus on being a good head teacher. I reflected on this and spoke with the commentator; they told me that although it is good to fight for a better education, I was being one-sided by doing this from a party political stance. They wanted me to be neutral and address the facts of the issue. This was incredibly useful advice, which I took on board, and I now believe that I can work across the party political landscape far better for it. I can see and understand the Pygmalion effect of Michael Gove's policies from 2010 to 2014 even now, and though I was openly critical at the time there is no doubt that those high expectations did improve outcomes for children. Whether I like it or not, the quality of writing I see is better for it and teacher expectations are higher than I have ever known. I could write an essay on what I did not like, but I have learnt to look and listen to both sides far more carefully than I did when I automatically dismissed anything based on party political bias. The truth is you can get more done working with the political party currently running education than constantly bemoaning what you don't have. Through taking this stance, I am in a much better position to look at what has improved in the education system over time and benefit from this, rather than look at everything as being insufficient and feeling powerless.

And now you do what they told you

This is not to say I am a happy and mild-mannered head teacher. My long-suffering MP gets letters and invites on a regular basis. A two-page letter on school funding, demands on what will be done due to the rising cost of energy, requests for clarification on why children at my special school with Education and Health Care Plans are included in SATs data? A joke about how long the next Education Secretary will be in post. I usually send careful and balanced letters, acknowledging what has been done but what I see as needing to be done next. They are not very punk in content – more elevator soft jazz – but they are about holding those who can make a difference to account for what they are doing to tackle the important issues I see affecting my community. In truth, do I feel they make a difference? Probably not, but that is not why I write them. The rebellious punk in me does not care if I change attitudes here, it is about doing what I believe is the right thing to do. It is about looking in the mirror and liking what I see when I look for the head teacher.

Political momentum in education can seem one-sided. This is how it is and get on with it. There can be a sense of hoop jumping and ridiculous paperwork to justify elements of our day-to-day role. Therefore, I ask myself two questions when educational change comes my way:

1. Do I really have to do this?
2. Am I happy to do this?

If both answers are no, then I will not do it. If the answer to question one is yes, then I will look to find the least painful way of moving forward, taking the path towards the least irritation for those of us it affects. If I get a 'yes and no' answer that is usually interesting and I tend to focus the anger that this brings on doing it but on my terms. The most recent examples of this have been the botched National Tutoring programme (which is a yes if I want the funding and no if I want to run my curriculum without massive disruptions) and the introduction of the Early Career Teaching pathways (which is also a yes if I want teachers and no if I can't find ways to cover them for two years). These are two government schemes that I have huge issues with that if I wasted too much time on would cause a Krakatoa-like anger outburst that would make my daily job even more stressful than it already is. Therefore, in both cases I have looked to set up simple systems that cause the least resistance within my community but do what I have been asked to do. Although I have to do parts of these things, it is important that I do them the way that best suits my community. If these challenges go unaddressed, it is virtually impossible to thrive as a school leader. Survive, yes, but thriving is a different matter. To thrive we need to think and feel differently about the roles we have as leaders and we need to feel confident enough not to do what we think others want us to do.

Is love enough?

Though school leadership can feel lonely, a key part of making it through is finding the support of others. I am careful with how I describe the support we give or receive though. For me it is not love, it is something else.

I came from a council estate, a so-called deprived background. My mother was 16 when she gave birth to me, my father 18. Both left school with no qualifications but they worked hard to care for me and a few years later my brother. My mother tells a story about how when she was pregnant she was taken into a room at the hospital and forcefully told that she needed to have an abortion, that she was too young to have a child. My nan forced her way into this meeting and with my mother distraught said that it was her choice and if she wanted the baby, she would help her – which, thankfully, is what she did. I spent a lot of time at my nan's while my mother held down two jobs – cleaning the toilets along the seafront of Burnham-on-Sea, Somerset and working the summer season cleaning at a holiday camp, and later at a school. My father worked 12-hour night shifts and I rarely saw him. Both worked hard so that we were provided for. They had no advantages in life but they loved us and continuously thought about our basic needs. They were both very proud people and did not want kindness or donations from others (in fact they were often openly hostile towards it) – they just wanted the opportunity to work and get on with their lives. That pride instilled in me a hardworking, self-help ethic: I don't want your charity, or your love – I want you to help me to help myself. Too often I have seen what people think is love and support when in fact they are disempowering proud people and their communities through a philanthropic, big-hearted kick in the teeth. This is why I am very careful now in how I describe my community. I do not like the way we define a community by its deprivation, as though this will be enough to understand why it under-performs. I do not like how we are blind to the many amazing things our com-munities are beyond their financial standing; the way that we can easily look down on people because of status or wealth. At times, we seem to be in love with a romantic notion of a Dickensian narrative where we are the saviours of the pitiful and desperate. I am not ignoring the terrible circumstances some families find themselves in. As I write this, I feel like I come across as more heartless than I would like, especially at a time when fuel and food poverty is higher than ever. I am not saying that I do not understand, care or help with these financial situations (I do), but I *am* saying that as leaders in our com-munity we need to think about the longer-term impact that any help we offer has. One-off support in certain situations can be a lifeline, but ultimately we all need help and support to become independent of needing help. Isn't that the ultimate goal? And therefore, how is our love enabling this rather than fuelling helplessness?

I have heard it said that you could run a school on love. It is a noble aim but I think it is wrong. When I read the dictionary definition of the word or relate it to my personal experiences and understanding, I find that it is not the right one for me in a school context. Love comes in many guises and having an under-standing of what this means within your leadership is important. For me, love is consistency and doing the right thing even when it hurts to do it. It has more in common with the word 'care' – *the provision of what is necessary for the health, welfare, maintenance and protection of someone or something* – than 'love' – *an intense feeling of deep affection*. When I look back at the mistakes that I have made in leadership I often find that I am trying to show love and understanding because I am too afraid to do the hardest parts of caring in the situation. I am trying to offer emotional support when actionable help is what is needed, and often to get the help it may *seem like I do not care*. Phoning social services when a family is in crisis is a form of love, not accepting violent behaviour is a form of love, respecting your community but expecting the best from it is a form of love, but none of this is enough if you do not set out to help people to help themselves.

Early into my headship journey I took a phone call that even as I write, almost 20 years later, I struggle to comprehend. It involved someone closely connected to my school community acting out of character and eventually a week later taking their own life. I had no idea that this surreal conversation would lead to such a terrible conclusion. That phone call was most likely a cry for help from someone who did not know how to ask for it. This one, five-minute moment still echoes through my memories. Over the years, I have had to come to many conclusions about it, most importantly that at the time I did not have the power, knowledge or skills to have stopped it, or make a critical difference. In truth, it is very unlikely I do today. It has taken me almost 20 years to realise this and I still hear that voice and play out that strange conversation in my head. I remember phoning their partner and trying to convey my concern without finding the words and saying what was just out of reach on the fringes of my consciousness. I remember being concerned but too afraid to mention mental health. I have now reached a point where I do not think 'What if I said this, or did that?.' I still remember the moment I found out the terrible news that they had killed themself. The rebel in me would take that phone call very differently now. I would not be scared to say 'I'm worried about you'.

I cannot count the number of times in my career where I have been face to face with someone whose emotional state had totally crumbled away because life had turned difficult or even cruel. People who have punched out, run over family members (or their pets), made successful or unsuccessful attempts at taking their life, hurt their child (or someone else's child), hurt themselves, lost a loved one, turned to drugs and alcohol, become bankrupt, broken the law, were sectioned or hated me and hated the world. Time and time again, I have been in situations like these, and when reflecting on them and looking at the positive changes that happened, almost always the ability to understand what was going wrong and to speak about it honestly seems to have been a vital factor in moving from helplessness to something much more empowering – the ability to find a way to be open and honest with people about what they need to do to go from one place they don't want to be to another place where they have their control back again. Speaking truth is a powerful thing and it needs a certain mindset to do it without fear. One of the greatest lessons is knowing that love is not about just giving – it is about learning to allow others to know how to give to themselves and those around them. It is about listening and being able to speak your truth in any situation. Being the rebel in the room is often a very good way of going about this. A true leader must be able to walk that line and not become another cog in the wheel of a system that if ignored can be anything but helpful for far too many communities.

Tame your ego

Other head teachers say I am egotistical – but enough about them ...

I have come to realise that head teachers are often the worst people to invite to a party. This may be because we live a life where the decisions we make put us at the centre of our schools and our communities. The world seems to revolve around us from morning to night, and all too often it can go to our head. I have had moments with head teachers who believe they are something special: 'I'm a star, goddamn it, I'm a superstar!'

When we live in a world where so much depends on us it can be all too easy to lose focus and become engulfed by our ego. This can quickly inflate our sense of self and self-importance. I have fallen for this on occasions, putting myself in for awards – it is very rare that you are awarded something without actually entering it. This is not necessarily a bad thing, but if you really do think you are 'the best head teacher in the world' then it probably shows how little you know about the role. Some of the best head teachers I know stay out of the spotlight. They know that getting attention does not mean you know more about running an effective school.

Yet, to survive, many head teachers have to find ways to tame their ego while believing in themselves and their ability to lead a school. They cannot lose their identity but also cannot allow it to overpower the needs of their school community. I have seen too many narcissistic school leaders become obsessed with their own super powers, watching their star rise and then, inevitably, come crashing down. Those who last through leadership learn to get this balance right. They are just as damning of their abilities as they are confident. They do not buy into the rhetoric. They know that with compromise there is often a very heavy price to pay, whether that is hidden feelings of guilt or remorse, or a diminishment in the way in which others see them. Hence, they develop personal practices that keep bringing them back to their core and the reasons as to why they are in education. These practices keep them sane and prevent them from betraying their values and what they believe in.

Conclusion: I did it my way

There is no one way to lead in a school. It is a spectacular odyssey of experiences that build on one moment after another. Lessons learnt through failure and success. Painful experiences alongside moments of hope and joy. Knowledge gained through sweat, blood and tears. Even as I look back over the chapters in this book, I realise that I have not touched on so many aspects of the role, but after nearly 20 years of leading in schools I can look back and know that I loved every second, every late-night governors' meeting, questioning parent, government initiative, boring policy and School Development Plan. I will be sad when I finally shut the office door one last time and walk away from the buzz of doing something that has enriched my life so much. Something that has felt so important and timeless.

At the beginning of 2023, I made a national newspaper headline stating that I had resigned because of the state of education. The interview had got me at a particularly low point and I was feeling very strongly about the lack of X, Y and Z in the education system. As I edit this now, I know nothing has really changed in my heart. I still love this job and as my father used to say, "Every job is difficult, Brian. Try getting up at 4am to milk the cows in a freezing February snow storm".

Being a head teacher should never be something that we see as a poisoned chalice within education, it should be an honour and an ambition for everyone who wants the best for others and their community. I sometimes, rather weirdly, picture my time in headship through the lens of film; the director shouts 'action' and the camera pulls back from the square of safety glass looking into the head's office. The head teacher, head in hands trying to grasp the enormity of their responsibility, the camera speeds down busy corridors vibrant and purposeful, past lessons full of focus and wonder, out across playgrounds buzzing with children laughing and happy and through the school gates; parents waiting, meeting, chatting and making friends – a community together, happy and vibrant. This moment in any school day is worthy of a film; it is epic and we must never forget this.

Everything I have written somehow seems inadequate, but maybe that is the reason that being a head teacher is such an amazing job. You can do it for years and feel like you are just beginning. Yes, it is, at times, mystifying, challenging, frustrating and terrifying. It is also magnificent, satisfying and joyous. Oh, and if you are lucky you get your own parking space.

As the head teacher, you only need to understand that it is never about power and always about service. You are a warden, protector, keeper, steward, overseer and custodian, but most importantly, you are someone who can really make a difference to other people's lives – an agent of hope who may end up as a sentence or paragraph in someone's Book of Legends. Being a head teacher is about the ripples you create that continue well beyond the final time you switch off your office light and shut the door. It is about having an ambition for a community and trying to build something to make other people's lives better. Ultimately, like all lessons in life, you need to embrace the adventure of it all and know that by being the leader you will be lucky enough to reflect upon a life well lived.

Index

Page numbers in *italics* refer to figures; page numbers in **bold** refer to tables.